Cambridge Elements

Elements in the Philosophy of Martin Heidegger
edited by
Filippo Casati
Lehigh University
Daniel O. Dahlstrom
Boston University

HEIDEGGER ON BEING AFFECTED

Katherine Withy
Georgetown University

CAMBRIDGE
UNIVERSITY PRESS

Shaftesbury Road, Cambridge CB2 8EA, United Kingdom

One Liberty Plaza, 20th Floor, New York, NY 10006, USA

477 Williamstown Road, Port Melbourne, VIC 3207, Australia

314–321, 3rd Floor, Plot 3, Splendor Forum, Jasola District Centre,
New Delhi – 110025, India

103 Penang Road, #05–06/07, Visioncrest Commercial, Singapore 238467

Cambridge University Press is part of Cambridge University Press & Assessment,
a department of the University of Cambridge.

We share the University's mission to contribute to society through the pursuit of
education, learning and research at the highest international levels of excellence.

www.cambridge.org
Information on this title: www.cambridge.org/9781009504041

DOI: 10.1017/9781009504058

First published 2024

A catalogue record for this publication is available from the British Library.

ISBN 978-1-009-50404-1 Hardback
ISBN 978-1-009-50409-6 Paperback
ISSN 2976-5668 (online)
ISSN 2976-565X (print)

Heidegger on Being Affected

Elements in the Philosophy of Martin Heidegger

DOI: 10.1017/9781009504058
First published online: May 2024

Katherine Withy
Georgetown University

Author for correspondence: Katherine Withy, kaw84@georgetown.edu

Abstract: Things get to us. We are moved or affected by 'things' in the ordinary sense – the paraphernalia of our daily lives – and also by ourselves, by others, and by ontological phenomena such as being and time. How can such things get to us? How can things matter to me? Heidegger answers this question with his concepts of finding (*Befindlichkeit*) and attunement (*Stimmung*). This Element explores how being finding allows things to matter to us in attunements such as fear and hope by allowing those things to show up as benefits or detriments to our pursuits and so to put those pursuits at stake. It also explores how we can be affected ontologically – that is, affected by being – in special attunements such as angst and boredom, as well as how Heidegger's account of being affected has contributed to our understanding of emotions, moods, and affective disorders.

Keywords: Heidegger, mood, attunement, angst, boredom

ISBNs: 9781009504041 (HB), 9781009504096 (PB), 9781009504058 (OC)
ISSNs: 2976-5668 (online), 2976-565X (print)

Contents

Method of Citation

All references to Heidegger's writings are to the standard edition of *Being and Time* (*Sein und Zeit*) or to the respective volume of the *Complete Edition* (*Gesamtausgabe*) of his writings. References to *Sein und Zeit* are cited as 'SZ' followed by the page number, e.g., 'SZ: 15'; references to volumes of the *Gesamtausgabe* are cited as 'GA' followed by the volume number, colon, and page number, e.g., 'GA55: 19'. Most English translations include the pagination of the German original, making it possible to dispense with citing the translations' pagination. Any exceptions are flagged in footnotes, in which case the German pagination is given followed by a slash and the pagination of the English translation, e.g., 'GA9: 106/84'. A full list of these primary texts can be found at the beginning of the References section.

> The world in which I find myself gets to me (*Die Welt, in der ich mich befinde, geht mich an*).
>
> Heidegger, *Grundbegriffe der aristotelischen Philosophie*

1 Introduction

1.1 The World Gets to Me

Things get to us. They affect, afflict, strike, matter to, and move us. We are moved or affected by 'things' in the ordinary sense – the paraphernalia of our daily lives – but also by ourselves, by others, and by ontological phenomena such as being and time. All of these things are able to get to us. How can they do that?

On this question, Martin Heidegger thinks that the history of philosophy has offered 'nothing essentially new' since Aristotle (GA20: 393; SZ: 139).[1] Aristotle addresses the question of how something can get to or happen to us when he discusses the *pathē*. He gives four definitions of '*pathos*' in the *Metaphysics* (*Met.* V XXI 1022b15–22), which Heidegger glosses:

(i) a quality of a substance that is open to change; 'this definition characterizes an entity as something that can in some way be affected by something. Something can *happen* to such an entity' (GA18: 194); it is open to 'becoming-otherwise' and has 'the character of alterability' (GA18: 195);

(ii) that change realised;

(iii) such changes that are hurtful or harmful; '[t]hat which happens to me is harmful in its happening. … But *pathos* is defined still more precisely: harmfulness is related mostly to *lupē* [pain], so that, as a result *my attunement [Stimmung] to this occurring affects me*. It is a becoming-relevant [*Angegangenwerden*] of something' (GA18: 195);

(iv) '[e]xtreme cases of benefit and suffering' (*Met.* V XXI 1022b21–22, trans. mod).

So, to experience a *pathos* is, most basically, to be impacted and changed by the world. For instance, the stone darkens when it gets wet. Any entity with suitable properties is subject to *pathē* understood in this sense. But, as we see in (iii) and (iv), some entities can be impacted in a distinctive way. They are not merely changed but helped or hurt. Those are the entities that are *in* the world.

---

[1] I quote from Macquarrie and Robinson's translation of *Being and Time*, with frequent modification. In quoting from this and other English translations, I consistently substitute 'entity' for 'being' (*Seiende*), decapitalise 'Being' (*Sein*), substitute 'angst' for 'anxiety' and 'dread' (*Angst*), substitute 'ability-to-be' for 'potentiality-for-being' (*Seinkönnen*), and transliterate all ancient Greek. I also modify translations for terminological consistency (especially regarding '*Befindlichkeit*' and '*Stimmung*'), to correct errors, and occasionally for the sake of emphasis, euphony, or gender neutrality.

Entities that are *in* the world can be impacted by things in such a way that they are moved or touched (cf. SZ: 54–5). They experience things as affecting them and themselves as affected by things. It is presumably by experiencing oneself as thus affected that one counts as hurt, or the opposite. The effect can be either positive or negative. When things impact me negatively, I am pained. When things impact me positively, I experience pleasure. The corresponding *pathē* can thus be sorted into, most immediately, the pleasant (*hēdu*) and the painful (*lupēron*), and also the beneficial (*sumpheron*) and the harmful (*blaberon*) (GA18: 47), the uplifting or upsetting, and so the elevated or depressed (GA18: 47, 49, 168, 185; GA20: 351). In these pairs, the latter are to be avoided and the former are to be pursued. So the things that I encounter can be categorised, generally, as either objects of avoidance or objects of pursuit (*Nicomachean Ethics* (*Eth. Nic.*) 1104b30–3; GA18: 280).

I thus find myself in the midst of objects of pursuit and avoidance, liable to impact from them. They can help or hurt, uplift or upset – and, correspondingly, I can be helped or harmed, uplifted or upset, pleased or pained. Not only do things show up to me as able to touch and move me in these ways, I show up to myself as vulnerable to being affected by them – or, as actually affected by them. Every *pathos* that I experience reveals me to myself as moved in some way, positioned and posed by the things I encounter.

It is because we are buffeted about by the world in this way that we ask one another, 'How is it going? *Wie geht's?*' (GA18: 244); '*Wie befinden Sie sich?* How do you find yourself?'. How are you faring, amidst the things that get to you? How have they moved you and so positioned you among them? Aristotle calls how we are positioned by things a *diathesis*, 'disposition' (*Met.* 1022b1–4; cf. Withy, 2015b: 23; Hadjioannou, 2013). To find ourselves so moved is to experience a *pathos* or what Heidegger calls a *Stimmung* (attunement) (Withy, 2021b). And being open to finding ourselves so attuned or disposed is what Heidegger calls *Befindlichkeit* (finding).

1.2 *Befindlichkeit* and *Stimmung*

In *Being and Time* (1927), *Befindlichkeit* is one of three structures that account for our openness to meaning and mattering (SZ §29). (The other two are understanding (*Verstehen*) and talk (*Rede*).) *Befindlichkeit* is that dimension of our openness by which we find ourselves affected by things that get to us or matter to us (*angehen*). It has to do with finding (*finden*), receptivity, passivity, dependence, situatedness, determinateness, and the past, as well as affects (feelings, emotions, moods). Precisely what it has to do with these and in what way is what is up for grabs in interpreting Heidegger's take on affectivity.

In particular, one's sense of what phenomena are at stake depends in large part on how, and how closely, one ties *Befindlichkeit* to emotions and moods.

Heidegger introduces *Befindlichkeit* in *Being and Time* by writing: 'what we indicate *ontologically* by the term "*Befindlichkeit*" is *ontically* the most familiar and everyday sort of thing; our *Stimmung*, our being-attuned [*Gestimmtsein*]' (SZ: 134; GA20: 353). This makes clear that *Stimmung* (attunement) is an ontic phenomenon, having to do with entities, whereas *Befindlichkeit* is an ontological phenomenon, having to do with being. Or rather: *Stimmung* is an existentiell phenomenon, having to do with how we concretely live out our lives as the existing entities that we are, while *Befindlichkeit* is an existential phenomenon, having to do with what it is (what it means, what it takes) to *be* the sort of existing entities that we are. The passage suggests, further, that we can understand what *Befindlichkeit* is by looking at its manifestations in *Stimmungen*.

In their translation of *Being and Time*, John Macquarrie and Edward Robinson translate *Stimmung* as 'mood': 'what we indicate *ontologically* by the term "*Befindlichkeit*" is ontically ... our mood' (SZ: 134). Understanding *Stimmungen* as moods fits well enough with an understanding of Aristotle's *pathē* as affects, feelings, or emotions. It makes good sense of Heidegger's focus on phenomena such as fear (SZ §30) (although, as interpreters point out (e.g., Freeman, 2016: 252), fear is usually classed as an emotion rather than a mood). But this interpretation and translation leads readers to receive Heidegger's account of affectivity as a contribution to the philosophy of mood and emotion and to hear the passage I quoted as claiming that what we ordinarily call 'mood' is the one and only manifestation of *Befindlichkeit*. I think, however, that the point in the passage is better put more carefully and capaciously – perhaps as John Haugeland (2013: 144) put it: 'mood and attunement are ... illustrative ontical manifestations of' *Befindlichkeit*. What we ordinarily call 'moods' are ontic manifestations of *Befindlichkeit* and they illustrate its features well. But that does not mean that we can take our direction from the phenomenon of mood. There may be other manifestations of finding that look different from mood, and it will not be immediately obvious *which* are those features of mood that best illustrate the phenomenon of *Befindlichkeit*. Further, we may be misled in what we find salient in moods by traditional philosophical and psychological approaches to the affects. For these reasons, we need to be flexible when we think of ontic manifestations of *Befindlichkeit*. To aid this flexibility, I translate *Stimmung* not as 'mood' but as 'attunement'.

'Attunement' has the additional benefit of picking up on some of the resonances of *Stimmung* that 'mood' does not. *Stimmung* can mean *atmosphere*, *disposition*, or *tuning*. As Macquarrie and Robinson note, it 'originally means the tuning of a musical instrument'.[2] Heidegger himself uses musical and atmospheric language, saying that a *Stimmung* is like 'a melody that does not merely hover over the so-called proper being at hand of the human, but that sets the tone for such being, i.e., attunes [*stimmt*] and determines [*bestimmt*] the manner and way of its being' (GA29/30: 101); or 'an atmosphere [*Atmosphäre*] in which we first immerse ourselves in each case and which then attunes us through and through [*durchstimmt*]' (GA29/30: 100). Because *Stimmung* has this immersive sense, it can extend beyond the individual, as Hubert L. Dreyfus (1991: 169) puts it, to 'refer to the *sensibility* of an age (such as romantic), the *culture* of a company (such as aggressive), the *temper* of the times (such as revolutionary), as well as the *mood* in a current situation (such as the eager mood in the classroom) and, of course, the mood of an individual' (cf. Blattner, 2006: 82–3). Put differently, *Stimmung* has to do with what in English we might call 'vibes', as in *the vibe of the party*, or *picking up on someone's vibes*. 'Vibe', of course, shortens 'vibration' and appropriately implies both an individual resonating with their situation and the situation's own atmosphere, to which those within it are attuned.

Stimmungen are whatever ways of vibing with the situation *Befindlichkeit* makes possible. '*Befindlichkeit*' is even more controversial and harder to translate than *Stimmung* (for discussion, see, e.g., Slaby, 2021: 243–4). Some interpreters prefer to leave it untranslated, as I have been doing. All agree that one translation is out of the question: that by Macquarrie and Robinson in their English translation of *Being and Time* – namely, 'state-of-mind'.[3] As Charles Guignon (2003 (1984): 184) explains, this transition is 'completely misleading', since *Befindlichkeit* 'is neither a "state" nor does it pertain to a "mind"'. *Befindlichkeit* is a term constructed to echo the phrase '*Wie befinden Sie sich?*' (literally, 'How do you find yourself?'; 'How are you?'). As Jan Slaby (2021: 243) points out, however, 'the dominant literal meaning of *sich befinden* is first of all, and quite simply: *being somewhere* – being located or situated, as in, for instance, "Ich befinde mich in Paris" ("I am in Paris")'. We can hear in 'finding' both that I find myself situated in Paris *and* that I find myself faring somehow in Paris.

The proposed translations of *Befindlichkeit* shuttle between emphasising one or the other of these senses but never quite manage both. They also succeed more or less well in avoiding the connotations of psychological interiority to which Macquarrie and Robinson's translation fell prey. What they fail at, by and large, is crafting neologisms that sound like English words. Colloquially, and somewhat literally, Robert Stolorow (2014: 8) offers 'how-one-finds-oneself-ness' and Dreyfus (1991: 168) at one time went fully colloquial with 'where-you'

---

re-at-ness'. As he notes, however, 'this leaves out the sensitivity to the situation' (Dreyfus, 1991: 168). This sensitivity is picked up by Guignon's (2003 (1984): 184) 'situatedness', but as Haugeland (2013: 34n26) points out, this translation leaves out the idea of *finding* oneself situated. Joan Stambaugh (1996: xv) opts for 'attunement' in her translation of *Being and Time* (and Matthew Ratcliffe (2008: 47) follows her), but of course this overlaps with the translation of *Stimmung* as 'attunement' and so leads to confusion between *Stimmung* and *Befindlichkeit*. Stambaugh (1996: xv) reportedly considered but rejected 'disposition' on the grounds that it is too psychological in connotation. Dreyfus and Haugeland both reject 'disposition' for the opposite reason: it is 'too outer' 'because of its use by behaviorists as disposition to behave' (Dreyfus, 1991: 168); not only does it 'misleadingly evoke[] reductive, behaviorist doctrines, . . . it misses the point that one finds oneself so disposed' (Haugeland, 2013: 143n8).

To avoid the association with behaviourism, Daniel O. Dahlstrom (2001: 295n84) adopts 'disposedness', a term that is also used by William Blattner (2006: 79), Taylor Carman (2003: 192), and Theodore Kisiel (1993: 492). Kisiel uses both 'disposition' and 'disposedness', which together capture us as situated or positioned *in* a context and so situated or positioned *by* it (compare Aristotle's '*diathesis*'). Christos Hadjioannou (2019a: 94) argues that 'disposition' 'conveys the sense of situatedness in an environing world, and also has the sense of finding-ness (being disposed is how one finds oneself "available")'. Slaby (2021: 244; cf. 2017: 9) agrees that '*disposedness* is excellent for getting at the conceptual range of *Befindlichkeit* and at its temporal logic' but he also likes 'findingness' as a translation, which 'while understandably shunned by language purists, drives home the sense of *radical situatedness* that Heidegger wishes to invoke'. I believe that 'findingness' comes from Haugeland (2013: 143, 196n4), who also earlier offered – as 'contrived rendition[s] of Heidegger's contrived word' (Haugeland, 2000: 52) – 'so-foundness' (Haugeland, 1989: 51) and 'sofindingness' (Haugeland, 2000: 52). While 'findingness' (or 'findliness') is the more literal translation, I translate *Befindlichkeit* as 'finding'. I also frequently leave it untranslated.

This Element, however, is titled *Heidegger on Being Affected*. Why this term, and why not use it to translate *Befindlichkeit*? 'Affectedness' is Dreyfus's preferred translation of *Befindlichkeit* in his *Being-in-the-World* (albeit 'without great enthusiasm' (1991: x)), since it 'at least captures our being already affected by things' (1991: 168). Steven Crowell (2013: 70) also chooses 'affectedness'. Dahlstrom (2001: 295n84) worries that this term refers to something too inner. I agree – if we hear 'affect' in the way that Haugeland (2013: 145–6) does: 'moods and attunements are the basic ways in which intraworldly entities *affect* us. This does not mean causing effects "in" us but rather eliciting affective responses from us.' Focusing on our inner affective responses to the world is indeed a problem, since it leaves out not only our situatedness but also the fact that it is our situation and the things in it that affect us, impact us, move us. But I do not think that this is a reason to reject the vocabulary of affectivity. While an *affect* may (on the standard definition) be an inner state or condition, *to be affected* (on any definition) is to be impacted by things, moved by things. (Similarly, etymologically, an e-motion is a matter of being moved.)

And it is clearly this being affected that Heidegger is interested in. He writes of sensing (another potential mode of *Befindlichkeit*, in addition to mood) that

> only because the 'senses' belong ontologically to an entity whose kind of being is findingly-being-in-the-world [*befindlichen In-der-Welt-seins*] can they be 'touched' [*gerührt*] by anything or 'have a sense for' something in such a way that what touches them shows itself in an affect [*Affektion*]. Under the strongest pressure and resistance, nothing like an affect would come about, and resistance itself would remain essentially undiscovered, if findingly-being-in-the-world [*befindliches In-der-Welt-sein*] had not already submitted itself to having entities within-the-world 'matter' to it in a way which its *Stimmungen* have outlined in advance. *Existentially, Befindlichkeit implies a disclosive 'submission' to the world, out of which we can encounter something that matters to us*. (SZ: 137–8)

It is because we are findingly in-the-world that we can be touched, moved, or stirred (*gerührt*, also: churned, mixed, agitated) by things, and so attuned to and by them in *Stimmungen*, including affects, emotions, moods, and sensations. What Heidegger is trying to get at through his concepts of *Befindlichkeit* and *Stimmung* is precisely this phenomenon: our being affected by things, or the fact that things get to us.

I, too, will try to get at the phenomenon of being affected, and I will do so by offering an interpretive reconstruction – largely in my own voice – of Heidegger's concepts of *Befindlichkeit* and *Stimmung*. I begin with *Befindlichkeit*, our openness to being moved by things (Section 2). I then show how we are moved in various *Stimmungen*, primarily moods, and including *Grundstimmungen* or ground-attunements (Section 3). I will conclude by considering the criticisms that Heidegger's insights have received and the contributions that they have made to various discussions (Section 4).

2 *Befindlichkeit*

The question of affectivity is: How can things *get to* me (*geht mich an*)? '*Angehen*' is translated in the English translations of *Being and Time* as 'to matter', as in: How can things *matter* to me? Heidegger gives the short answer: 'The fact that this sort of thing' – that is, entities that are 'unserviceable, resistant, or threatening' – 'can "matter" … is grounded in *Befindlichkeit*' (SZ: 137). The slightly longer answer is that things matter to me insofar as they show up as benefits or detriments to my pursuits and put those pursuits at stake. The even longer and full answer requires reconstructing Heidegger's accounts of the ready-to-hand, the world, finding, understanding, and talking from Division I of *Being and Time*. These accounts together show how we are *in* the world in such a way that things can show up to us as both meaningful and mattering. In this section, I give a short version of that longer answer.

2.1 Meaning and Mattering

Let me begin with the fact that entities are meaningful. To say that entities are meaningful is to say that they show up to us intelligibly in the context of what we are doing. We encounter entities first of all not as objects but as paraphernalia that we 'deal with', 'manipulate', and 'put to use' (SZ: 66–7) when we are 'at work' (SZ: 70). These entities are 'ready-to-hand' to be put to work in our projects. To be ready-to-hand is for an entity to show up as offering opportunities for us to engage with it. The entity affords us opportunities to act. *What* opportunities for acting the entity offers to us determines what it is. Thus, something that affords *protecting from the rain* is (depending on precisely how it affords that) a shelter or an umbrella (or a raincoat, awning, tarpaulin, etc.), and something that affords *transiting affordably and publicly* is (depending on how precisely it affords that) a bus or a train (etc.). Heidegger speaks of the table, door, carriage, and bridge (SZ: 149), which afford (something like) *placing things on, entering or exiting through, riding in*, and *crossing over*, respectively. It is by affording these ways of engaging with them that those entities show up meaningfully to us *as* tables, doors, carriages, bridges, buses, bus stops, and umbrellas.

The vocabulary of 'affording' comes from the psychologist J. J. Gibson (1986), who speaks of the affordances that entities and the environment present to embodied agents. Mark Wrathall (2021b) has argued that it is Gibson's concept of affordance that Heidegger aims to capture with his term *'Bewandtnis'* ('involvement', 'relevance') in *Being and Time*. *Bewandtnis* is the being of entities ready-to-hand (SZ: 84): that by virtue of which they are what they are. The translations 'involvement' and 'relevance' have the benefit of stressing that what an entity affords, and so what it is, depends on how it is implicated in (i.e., involved in, relevant to) our pursuits. But Gibson builds this into his account of affordances, too: an entity only affords what it affords in conjunction with what we are doing and our ability to do that. Thus, a bus stop affords waiting to catch the bus only to someone with the savvy to navigate the public transit system, who has the physical and financial capacities to do so, and who is in the business of getting from A to B by public transit. For someone who does not know the system, is materially unable to participate in it, and/or does not move around town, the bus stop does not offer itself up as a place from which to catch the bus.

Thus, Wrathall (2021b: 31) writes: 'Affordances are a function of, on the one hand, the projects, abilities, skills, and dispositions of the specific agent and, on the other hand, the possibilities furnished by the equipment the agent encounters.'

By affording, entities show up meaningfully as what they are. But they do not yet matter to or move us. To do this, things must not only offer opportunities for engaging with them, they must 'call out for' our engagement. The bus stop cries, 'Sit here and wait for the bus!'; when it begins to drizzle, the rain says, 'Avoid me or else I will ruin your books!'; the umbrella calls, 'Open me! Open me!' (or, if you prefer, think of a cool drink on a hot day: 'Drink me!'). When entities call out in this way, they are not merely intelligible or meaningful; they matter. This is how ready-to-hand entities move entities like us: not by effecting changes in our properties but by insisting upon certain types of engagement with them. They 'might appear to me as urgent or pressing, safe or threatening, interesting or boring, easy, difficult or impossible, predictable or unpredictable, achievable without effort, beyond my control, and so on' (Ratcliffe, 2013: 158).[4] We are 'constantly being ... solicited and summoned [*angegangen*]' (GA20: 351) by things. The umbrella moves me to open it; the rain demands that I act to protect my books; the bus stop beckons with the promise of the bus's imminent arrival. I am now waiting for the bus with my umbrella open against the rain, newly disposed in the world. Entities have gotten to me.

When this happens, the entity's affordings (*Bewandtnisse*) are solicitings, in which the entities call, demand, or move us to engage with them.[5] Solicitings arise when what entities offer corresponds to my needs or desires – to stay dry, to protect my books, to get home quickly. So, like affordings, solicitings are relational rather than independent features of entities. It is not that we tune into the calls of entities so much as that their calls sound only for our attuned ears. Thus a soliciting is not something that I reveal or discover in an entity but

---

[4] Ratcliffe does not draw the distinction between affording and soliciting in the way that I do (Section 2.2) because he thinks that only finding and not understanding is world-disclosing (2008, 47–8). He also rejects Gibson's notion of affordances as inadequate to the phenomenon (Ratcliffe, 2015: 61n24). But he gives terrific examples of soliciting:

> Entities present themselves as enticing, functional, relevant to our current projects, threatening, urgent, interesting, offering pleasure, and so on. These broad categories of mattering encompass a range of further subcategories. For instance, not everything is threatening in quite the same way, and a threat might be avoidable, unavoidable, determinate or indeterminate, imminent or distant. Other people appear to us as significant in further ways, as offering potential friendship, companionship, humiliation, conversation, assistance, approval and disapproval. (Ratcliffe, 2010: 603)

[5] Gibson does not use the vocabulary of 'soliciting' and he does not distinguish this concept from that of affording. He does, however, speak of 'valences' or 'invitation characters', which he takes as precursors to the concept of affordance (Gibson, 1986: 138).

something that arises when what I need and what the entity offers happen to align.

While the term 'soliciting' implies that the entity invites us to engage with it, entities can also solicit by repelling or repulsing us. That is: entities can matter in ways that are negatively rather than positively valenced. Some entities assist our pursuits and others harm or hinder them. Thus Aristotle's distinction between the pleasant and the painful, the beneficial and the harmful (see Section 1.1), Gibson's (1986: 143) distinction between entities that 'offer benefit or injury, life or death', and Heidegger's tendency to categorise ready-to-hand entities as either serviceable (usable, etc.) or detrimental (e.g., SZ: 83).[6] That which solicits with a positive valence is that which, broadly speaking, benefits or helps me in my pursuits, and that which solicits me with a negative valence is that which, broadly speaking, harms or impedes me in my pursuits. Attunements that tune me into the former are 'elevated' (e.g., hope (SZ: 345)) and those that tune me into the latter are 'depressed' (e.g., fear (SZ: 342; GA18: 131)) (GA18: 168, 185; GA20: 351).

So, *Befindlichkeit* is whatever it is that allows us to be attuned to how things matter or solicit, and this is our being moved by things. Being so affected goes beyond encountering entities as meaningful or intelligible and so as affording certain types of engagement. I said that meaningful things come to matter when the affording corresponds to our needs or desires. But that is not quite how Heidegger would tell the story of how mattering arises out of meaning.

2.2 Submitting to the World

Heidegger rightly insists in *Being and Time* that 'there "is" no such thing as *an* equipment' (SZ: 68). His point is that entities only afford what they afford in concert with other entities that offer complementary opportunities for engaging. For example, the bus stop can only afford what it affords if the bus affords what it affords, along with bus routes, fare cards, transit apps, bicycle lanes, and so on. Affordances are, as Wrathall (2021b: 32–3) puts it, 'contextually determined' – and, further, the entire context of affordances is itself determined by a 'purposive context'. Our purposes or pursuits coordinate with entities not only to allow particular entities to afford but to open up entire contexts or fields of interconnected possible ways in which things

---

[6] Heidegger is likely influenced in this both by Aristotle and by the phenomenologist Max Scheler, who takes us to be immediately open in our affective lives not only to the agreeable and the disagreeable but also to the noble and the vulgar, the beautiful and the ugly, the morally right and wrong, and the holy and the unholy (Schloßberger, 2020: 75). In *Being and Time*, Heidegger credits Scheler with insights regarding the affects and something like a distinction between affordances and solicitations ('acts which "represent" and acts which "take an interest"' (SZ: 139)).

can afford. Thus, it is by taking up a pursuit such as *navigating the city by public transit* that things can first come to count for me *as* buses and bus stops, fare cards, and bus routes. (The example that Heidegger gives is *providing shelter*, such as by building a house (SZ: 84).)[7] That taking up pursuits opens up fields of affordances is most clear when we first adopt (or surrender) some pursuit. We swap the ride share app for a bus card, or take up bicycling, or decide to walk to work, and a whole new world opens up, filled with new types of things. It is a world of ways in which things can be meaningful: 'the categorial whole of a *possible* interconnection of the ready-to-hand' (SZ: 144) and other modes of being (such as being another case of Dasein, the entity that we each are; see Withy (2019: 164)).

So we take up pursuits and thereby open worlds of possible ways in which things can be meaningful. Doing this is what Heidegger calls 'projecting' (*entwerfen*) and it is an expression of that dimension of our openness that Heidegger calls 'understanding' (*Verstehen*) (SZ §31). (Actually encountering entities as affording this or that, and so as being (intelligible as) this or that, is 'interpreting' (SZ: §32).) But understanding is always finding and finding is always understanding (SZ: 142; GA20: 356). In addition to *throwing forth* (*entwerfen*) a world, we also bring it back to (*züruckbringen auf*) (SZ: 340) ourselves. As finding, we submit to the world, and it is out of this submission that matterings or solicitings arise (SZ: 137–8).

Consider the rain. I am at the bus stop when it begins to drizzle. The drizzle suggests rain, and the imminent rain is intelligible to me in a variety of ways, according to the various projects I am undertaking. It is *moisture for the garden* (if I garden) but also it *will make me and my clothes wet* as well as *dampen my books*. These are ways in which the rain is meaningful in terms of my pursuits of *gardening*, of *arriving at work presenting appropriately*, and of *taking care of my books*. But to be so intelligible is not yet for the rain to matter; it does not yet say 'Avoid me! Avoid me!' (or, with the garden in mind, perhaps: 'Welcome me!'). In order to show up as *to be avoided* and so as (negatively) soliciting, the rain must draw close (SZ: 140) in the sense that it is 'awaited *right back to the*

---

[7] Note that pursuits such as *providing shelter* and *navigating the city by public transit* are activities that we carry out and that govern and organise a complex of subordinate activities (e.g., *nailing this beam to that*; *waiting at the bus stop*). They are that *for the sake of which* those other activities are carried out and so structure the practical context within which we live out our lives and in terms of which entities are intelligible. Such pursuits are perhaps Aristotelian *praxeis*. They are *not* practical identities or 'possible ways to be', such as *being a homemaker* (Dreyfus, 1991: 16) or *being a public transitter*. I have worked with the latter way of interpreting Dasein's 'projects' in my publications to date; in this Element, I try out the former. This approach more closely aligns with what Heidegger says in *Being and Time*, as well as with its Aristotelian inspiration in the discussion of that for the sake of which we act in the opening paragraphs of the *Nicomachean Ethics*.

entity which I myself am' in 'a letting-something-come-towards-oneself' such that it '*come*[*s*] *back* to one's factically concernful ability-to-be' (SZ: 341). (Or, as Heidegger writes of someone who hopes: 'He who hopes takes himself *with him* into his hope, as it were, and brings himself up against what he hopes for' (SZ: 345).) In other words, in order to matter, something must come all the way back to me: so close to me that it puts my pursuits at stake.

'Being at stake' is a gambling metaphor. 'The stake(s)' is the amount of money wagered on a horse race or card game and so at risk of being lost or won back. Something is at stake when its success or failure depends on a turn of events that is not within our control. Our affectivity (i.e., finding) subjects us to stakes of this sort, in a way that taking up our pursuits (i.e., understanding) by itself does not. Thus the rain might be relevant to taking care of my garden, and it might be relevant with either a positive or a negative valence, but only if it puts my garden and/or my pursuit of gardening at stake (to some degree or another) does it *threaten* and so matter as *to be avoided* (or if it is much-needed, *beckon* and so show up as *to be welcomed*).[8] So too, getting rained on when on the way to work might *make sense* in terms of how it impacts my *arriving at work presenting appropriately* but only insofar as it puts me at risk of failing in this pursuit does it show up as a threat to be avoided, sending me running for shelter or reaching for my umbrella.

The distinction between meaning and mattering can be difficult to grasp, since we do not often experience affordings in the absence of solicitings. (Imagine arriving at work soaking wet, aware that it looks bad but unmoved by that fact. This is some sort of breakdown in our affective life, perhaps one that is not dissimilar to angst (Section 3.2).) More often than not, the calls of solicitings are so quiet that they barely rise above the offers of affordings. Things just do not matter that much. In our day-to-day lives, the stakes are often neither particularly high nor particularly low and so nothing much is at risk. The soliciting of things is muted. ('Eh', says the umbrella, 'you could open me?') Our affective lives are accordingly dull. Rather than the highs and lows of high-stakes wagers we experience 'the pallid lack of mood [*Ungestimmtheit*] – indifference – which is addicted to nothing and has no urge for anything, and which abandons itself to whatever the day may bring, . . . [j]ust living along in a way which "lets" everything "be" as it is' (SZ: 345) (see Section 3.1).

Nonetheless, the stakes could be high. We are at least open to being impacted strongly by things on which the fate of our pursuits rests. In this regard, our lives are less like the strategic games of chess to which they are often compared (e.g.,

---

[8] When it is not merely my garden but my pursuit of gardening as such that it at stake, I risk death (as a gardener) (see Withy, 2022a: 313f.).

Haugeland, 1989) and more like risky games of poker. From the perspective of our affective lives, we find our projects always at the mercy of entities that are not up to us. This is the flipside of the fact that we carry out our pursuits in concert with those entities. We thus depend on them and are vulnerable to them. Heidegger says that this follows from our facticity (i.e., our distinctive factuality): 'The concept of "facticity" implies that an entity "within-the-world" has being-in-the-world in such a way that it can understand itself as bound up in its "destiny" with the being of those entities which it encounters within its own world' (SZ: 56). We depend on other entities to live out our lives; we *need* them. This need makes us vulnerable – but it is also what allows things to matter. It is the Heideggerian version of the need that turns affordings into solicitings. It is not a biological, physiological, or psychological need but an ontological need: we carry out our lives *with* other entities, inescapably. We cannot do it alone.

Unlike the need or desire for a cool drink on a hot day, our ontological need for entities is not directed at this entity or that entity but at entire contexts of entities – indeed, the whole context of affordings that is relevant to our pursuits. When we take up some pursuit, we open a range of interconnected possible ways in which things can be relevant to our projects and so afford opportunities for engaging with them. When we 'submit[] to that world which is already disclosed' (SZ: 139) by our projecting, bringing those possibilities of affording back toward us and staking the success or failure of our pursuits on them, the field of possible affordings becomes a field of possible solicitings (see Withy, 2019). We open a world not just of meanings but of matterings. In light of that world, things can show up as *impediments, bolsters,* or *boosts* to our pursuits, as things that are *necessary* or *irrelevant, urgent* or *exciting* – or as *just another damn thing that we have to deal with.*

If our world of matterings is dominated by possible ways in which things can threaten and thwart us, our world will be a fearful and precarious one. If it is dominated by possible ways in which things can support and delight us, it will be a joyful and stable one. (And if it is dominated by *more damn things that we have to deal with,* it – and we – will be insufferable.) These are extremes, of course. Most of us inhabit worlds that are not so monochromatic. But the examples demonstrate the point: the constellation of possible solicitings in which we dwell makes for the tonality of our being-in-the-world. We sometimes capture this tonality by speaking of an individual's disposition: a sunny disposition, a fearful disposition, a dreary disposition. We can begin to grasp why the vocabularies of disposedness, vibes, tuning, and mood present themselves as ways of glossing the phenomenon of *Befindlichkeit.*

We have seen how, as finding, we open a world of possible ways in which things can matter, on the basis of which we can encounter particular things that matter.

I will return to the world-opening character of *Befindlichkeit* briefly in Section 2.4. But first, we need to consider how *Befindlichkeit* opens us to ourselves.

2.3 Finding Myself Thrown

In allowing entities to come so close to us that they put our pursuits at stake, we are revealed to ourselves. If our pursuits are at stake, then we are also at stake. We are at stake precisely because we are already committed to the pursuits that are at risk and because we depend on entities. We find ourselves thrown into being entities who pursue projects – and, entities who are pursuing *these particular* projects – in the midst of entities that we depend on and so entities that can put those pursuits at risk.

Thrownness (*Geworfenheit*) is the 'that it is' of our being as Dasein (SZ: 135): 'the fact "that it is, and that it has to be something with an ability-to-be as the entity which it is"' (SZ: 276, cf. SZ: 134, 284). (For more on thrownness, see Withy, 2014 and 2021c.) To be thrown is to be stuck with one's being and to have to go on from there – to have been, as it were, dealt a hand that one must play. To have been dealt such a hand is, first, to be already in the business of playing some particular type of game. For us, this is 'the game of life': the game of being Dasein, the entity who makes sense of things and is moved by things. It is, second, to have in front of one a particular set of cards, which one must take up and play out. This is a particular set of projects that I am pursuing, such as *taking public transit to work* and *arriving at work presenting appropriately* (and *being a professor* and *being a city-dweller* and so on). It is, third, to have to play out those cards or pursuits, for better or worse, in the context of whatever else may come up during the course of the game – whatever other cards or entities, bad deals or rain showers, one might encounter. (This is the connection between thrownness and facticity, which implies our dependence on entities other than ourselves.) As Haugeland (1989: 64) puts it, using the analogy of chess:

> [D]asein is somehow stuck with them [things] as they stand. The only way I can carry on with my game is by dealing with my current position, including your pawn and my rook; I cannot but deal with that position … because it is the position I find myself, so to speak, 'plunked down in'. For dasein [*sic*] in each case, the current situation is, inevitably, the first situation of the rest of its life.

In sum: we are thrown into some particular situation amidst entities, into pursuits to which we are already committed, and into our most basic project of being Dasein, the entity that we are.

When we open a world of possible solicitings by bringing the context of affordings back to ourselves, we bring that context of affordings back to our thrown being. Specifically, we bring it back to our thrownness into the project that we are pursuing. It is our pursuits that are put at stake by entities and so it is the fact that these are the pursuits that we pursue – and that we *are* pursuing them and *have* them to pursue – that is at risk. Just as staking one's savings on a horse race makes one profoundly aware of those savings as one's safety net, so too allowing entities to put my pursuits at stake opens me to my commitment to those pursuits as my way of leading my life. I find myself delivered over to and stuck with those pursuits, already and irreparably in the midst of playing out a hand that I cannot back out of and the dealing of which to me I can never undo.

That I find myself *already* in some situation reflects the fact that I experience my being stuck with a situation as a fait accompli. This is why finding myself thrown is associated with the past and especially with the (English) present perfect tense (e.g., *I have x'd*), which captures what in the past has already been accomplished yet impacts the present (Blattner, 2024: 230–3; Slaby, 2014; Freeman & Elpidorou, 2015). Of course, this does not mean that what was accomplished in the past was not, at that time, up to me. To be delivered over to my pursuits does not mean that I did not choose them myself (and so, as it were, deal my own hand). It was me, and not someone else, who decided to take public transit to work. (If I was forced into it by necessity or otherwise coerced, then it is not technically a *pursuit* or *project* of mine; it is merely something that I do.) At the same time, my opting for this particular pursuit was not a pure expression of free will; I opted for this pursuit because it struck me as worthwhile or valuable. This is an important point: the pursuits that I take up call me to them; they solicit me just as other entities do – and, like other entities, they solicit me in the context of other (positive and negative) solicitings, i.e., in the context of other pursuits that strike me as valuable or not valuable, of traits or capacities that seem worth developing or not, of things that others deem important or not, and so on (Blattner, 1999: 51–2). (In Withy (2019), I called this special class of solicitings 'vocational solicitings'.) On the basis of these solicitations, I commit to some pursuits and not others (and this is another way in which understanding is always finding (SZ: 142; GA20: 356)). But once I have taken up some pursuit, it is part of the situation that I am stuck with, from which I must start and with which I must deal. I have been thrown into it.

If I were not stuck with my pursuits they could not be at stake. They would merely come and go. And so when my pursuits are put at stake, I am opened to the fact that I am thrown into them. So in allowing things to matter by bringing the context of affordings back to me so as to put my pursuits at stake, *Befindlichkeit* brings me back to my thrownness – to my 'thrown being-in-the-world, which has been delivered over to itself in its being' (SZ: 189). Being so delivered, however, is a burden:

> To this entity it [a case of Dasein] has been delivered over, and as such it can exist solely as the entity which it is; and *as this entity* to which it has been thus delivered over, it *is, in its existing*, the basis of its ability-to-be. Although it has *not* laid that basis *itself*, it reposes in the weight of it, which is made manifest to it as a burden by Dasein's *Stimmung*. (SZ: 284)

Attunements reveal this 'manifest burden of being' (SZ: 134): the burden of being thrown into, and so stuck with, our being, with no choice but to start from where we are. But this burden can be revealed either by turning toward it or by turning away from it (SZ: 135). Our attunements usually reveal it 'in the manner of an evasive turning-away' (SZ: 136, original italicised) (since even turning away from something requires disclosing it (SZ: 135)). We evade the burden of our thrown being. Elation does this by 'alleviating' the burden (SZ: 135), making our being stuck seem liberating, while fear does it by distracting us from it: in fear, 'one has forgotten oneself and makes present a jumble of hovering possibilities' (SZ: 342). (Heidegger gives the example of a person in a burning house running around to save scattered, unimportant things (SZ: 342). Think also of the fearful poker player fixated on whether their cards are straight, or the giddy gambler who no longer seems to realise that they are losing their savings.) It remains to be theorised how and why different attunements turn away from or toward the burden of being. The important point is that, wherever they turn, all modes of *Befindlichkeit* reveal us to ourselves as thrown.

2.4 The Three Essential Characteristics of *Befindlichkeit*

Revealing us as thrown is 'the *first* essential characteristic of *Befindlichkeit*': it 'discloses Dasein in its thrownness, and – proximally and for the most part – in the manner of an evasive turning-away' (SZ: 136). '[T]he *second* essential characteristic of *Befindlichkeit*' is that it '*has already disclosed, in every case, being-in-the-world as a whole*' (SZ: 136–7). We have already seen how *Befindlichkeit* is world-disclosing, in opening up a field of solicitings out of the context of affordings. In this world-disclosing, *Befindlichkeit* is also self-disclosing: in bringing the context of affordings back to impact our pursuits, we find ourselves having been called to (finding) take up some pursuit (understanding), which we now find ourselves stuck with (being thrown, being finding), and the success or failure of which depends on other entities (being factical), which we also find ourselves stuck with (being thrown, being finding) and which thereby show up as mattering (being-absorbed, falling). This very last is our discovering entities. Thus we see how *Befindlichkeit* discovers entities, discloses world, and discloses ourselves – and how, in disclosing us to ourselves, it discloses us in the whole of our being-in-the-world as existing (understanding), being factical (and thrown, finding), and falling (being-absorbed). This very last is the third essential characteristic of *Befindlichkeit*: it allows entities to matter to us (SZ: 137–8). This is the point with which I began (in Section 2.1), and by returning to it we will see how *Befindlichkeit* explains such mattering.

'[T]he world which has already been disclosed beforehand' as a field of affordings in understanding and a field of solicitings in finding 'permits what is within-the-world to be encountered' (SZ: 137). We saw that the world disclosed as a field of solicitings might, for instance, be a joyful world or a fearful world. Heidegger calls dwelling in this latter, for example, our 'fearfulness' (*Furchtsamkeit*) (SZ: 141; GA20: 396). Such fearfulness 'has already disclosed the world, in that out of it something like the fearsome may come close' (SZ: 141). This is to say that, insofar as I am fearful, things can show up as threatening my projects – or as sources of respite or safety, as means of defence or avoidance, and so on. Such fearfulness is not an intentional emotion in which I encounter some particular entity that I fear, but instead the condition of possibility of that. It is what I would lack were I truly fearless: a disposition or attunement that first makes it possible to encounter things in terms of the threats that they pose. 'Only something which is in the *Befindlichkeit* of fearing (or fearlessness) can discover that what is environmentally ready-to-hand is threatening' (SZ: 137). The same is true for gladness (or joyfulness, *Freudigkeit*) (GA18: 54) and other such modes of finding. (Slaby (2010: 103) calls such modes of finding 'existential orientations'; Ratcliffe (2008: 49, 52) calls them 'feelings of being' or 'deep emotional states' (Ratcliffe 2010: 604) (but see Kush & Ratcliffe, 2018: 78, for a revised interpretation).)

Attunements such as fearfulness make possible attunements such as fearing, and both are made possible by *Befindlichkeit*. Being in an attunement such as fearfulness consists in opening a world with a particular range of interconnected ways in which entities can matter, which we do when we bring the field of affordings opened by our projects back to put our thrown being at stake. A more specific account of the ways in which entities can put our projects at stake will explain a more precise suite of affective possibilities – including possibilities of sensation and other nonmooded modes of *Befindlichkeit* (see Withy, 2019). I will not undertake such an account here, although I will consider some particular *Stimmungen* in the next section.

In this subsection, we have returned to the beginning by seeing how *Befindlichkeit* accounts for the fact that entities get to us. Or rather – we have seen how entities can get to *me*. I have yet to explain how they can get to *us*.

2.5 Being Affected with and by Others

Sometimes things get to me but often things get to *us*. This is clear from phenomena of communal *Stimmungen*, such as the *Zeitgeist*. Heidegger writes, for instance, of boredom as the mood of the age (GA29/30: 200) and later speaks of the 'ground-attunement . . . [of] a historical people in its entirety' (GA39: 80). He also writes about spending time with a person immersed in grief: 'He draws us into the manner in which he is, although we do not necessarily feel any grief ourselves' (GA29/30: 100). Or: 'A human being who – as we say – is in good humour brings a lively atmosphere with them. . . . Or another human being is with us, someone who . . . makes everything depressing and puts a damper on everything' (GA29/30: 100).

We usually understand phenomena of shared affectivity through the metaphor of contagion: an affect occurring in one subject escapes and infects others. But Heidegger does not think of affects as infectious because he does not think of them as interior in the first place. *Stimmungen* are not in us; we are in them (thus: 'I am in a mood'). It follows that we are not empathetic, in the sense that we do not project our own internal *pathē* into (*em-*) others, either in order to share our affects or in order first to connect with others (GA20: 334; SZ: 125; GA39: 89). But we are sympathetic, in the sense that we experience *pathē* together with (*sym-*) others. Experiencing *pathē* with others is one of our primordial ways of being-with others (GA18: 250; GA29/30: 100) (compare Scheler's concept of 'feeling-with-one-another' [*Miteinanderfühlen*] (Schloßberger, 2020: 79); Scheler also uses the example of grief). Our being-in-the-world is always a being-with-others (SZ: 114) and that means that our taking up pursuits is always in concert with or in the context of others, that finding ourselves is always finding ourselves thrown with and into the company of others, and that discovering entities is always a discovering with others and a discovering of others. It follows that we can find others as mattering in our *Stimmungen* ('Help me!' 'Love me!' 'Leave me alone!') and that we can experience *Stimmungen* together with others.

Often when we are attuned together, it is because we are each pursuing the same project (e.g., separately waiting for the bus, taking up gardening as a hobby) or pursuing a single project together (e.g., taking care of our garden, being friends). However we share it, our shared pursuit opens its own world of meanings and matterings, which we also share. Thus we will share a suite of affective possibilities and be put at stake by the same entities in the same ways. When we encounter those entities together, they will matter to us and we will be frightened or hopeful (or whatever) together. Things will get to *us*.

Such shared projects are almost certainly more common than we think. All, or almost all, of our pursuits are, in fact, also pursued by others or are pursued in concert with others. This is why shared and communal attunements are so common. Thus everyone trying to catch the bus to work frets together when the bus does not show up – and all are relieved together when it finally does show. Members of a sports team will together fear that the coming storm will make the ground too muddy to play on. Citizens of a democracy will worry collectively when the integrity of their elections is called into question. Most generally, we are plausibly engaged in global collective pursuits, such as *ensuring the continued survival and success of our species*, and in projects that all of us each pursue, such as *going about our individual lives as cases of Dasein*. The former leads (or should lead) us to collectively fear the climate catastrophe. The latter leads (or should lead) us each to fear perishing and/or demise. Insofar as we are always with others and in community, we share attunements.[9]

So far, I have spoken of shared attunements as arising from encounters in common with entities that put our shared pursuits at stake. But there are cases in which it is not just that things get to *us* but that what gets to me or us is *others*. Others can move us – and move us into the attunement that they are experiencing. If contagion is not the right metaphor for this – if we do not *pick up* or *catch* attunements, if they do not *infect* us – then how do attunements travel among us? How can others get to me, and in such a way that we come into a shared attunement?

We share things with others by talking. To talk is to be-with others: 'All talk [*Rede*] … [is] essentially being-with' (GA20: 362) and to be-with others is to speak with them. This is because being-with-others always goes along with being-in-the-world and being-in-the-world is disclosing, in part, by virtue of talk (*Rede*). Talking is an aspect of disclosing that is 'equiprimordial with *Befindlichkeit* and understanding' (SZ: 161, original italicised) such that, just as understanding is always finding and finding is always understanding, so too both are always talking (and vice versa).[10] 'This means that in any talking … Dasein itself and its *Befindlichkeit* are co-disclosed [*mitentdeckt*]' (GA20: 363). In talking, we share our modes of finding. (For more on this, see McMullin, 2006, 2013: ch. 6; Withy, 2021d.)

---

[9] There is more work to be done on how different ways of sharing attunements arise from different ways of being-with-others. Such work will have to reckon with Heidegger's example of the grieving person, whose grief affects us but does not lead us to share the attunement. The accounts that I give in this section all involve sharing attunements.

[10] Talking and finding do not appear to be equiprimordial in Heidegger's lectures on Aristotle, where he suggests that the *pathē* are 'the ground out of which speaking arises' (GA18: 262, original italicised), and in particular that fear or angst brings us to speaking (GA18: 261).

Imagine that someone at the bus stop says to you, 'Please, share my umbrella' (Gouldman, 1966). This instance of talking manifests four structural moments (SZ: 161–2; GA20: 363). It (i) speaks *about* something, namely, the umbrella, and (ii) *says* something of it, namely, that you are welcome to share it. But no offer to share shelter is ever quite so simple. In offering their umbrella, your cocommuter (iii) makes known – through, first of all, 'intonation, modulation, the tempo of talk, "the way of speaking"' (SZ: 162; GA20: 363) – what matters to and moves them in the situation. Are they eager to lend a helping hand or reluctant but offering under obligation? Are they a bibliophile worried about your books getting wet? Are they *flirting*? Their talking makes known 'the way in which [they are] currently finding (attuned) [*die Weise der Befindlichkeit (der Stimmung)*]' (SZ: 162). In this, they (iv) communicate with you – in the sense of sharing with you (L. *commūnicāre*, to share (with)) – how they find themselves disposed in the situation. If they *are* flirting with you, they are attuned to the situation as one filled with opportunities to (fail to) further intimacy. If the communication succeeds, you are now so attuned, too. The entire situation, and your position in it, has changed from one of dreary routine to one filled with either welcome or unwelcome (depending on your other pursuits and their matterings) romantic possibilities. Someone has gotten to you.

The work of sharing attunements is done by two elements of the talking: the manner of speaking and what is said of the entity. By speaking of the umbrella as a potential shared space of shelter, your cocommuter has oriented you toward the umbrella in a new and definite way – as a potential source of shelter and as a potential space in which love can grow. The talking has enacted a 'co-directedness toward the same thing' such that you are 'oriented to that situation as [they are]' (McMullin, 2006: 177). But it is not what is said that is doing the real work in this case; it is their tone and manner of speaking that lets you know that the speaker is flirting and that they are offering the umbrella-space as a site of potential intimacy. Indeed, it is not just their voice (*Stimme*) that makes known that they find themselves attuned (*gestimmt*) to the situation flirtatiously. Their body language also talks – the way they are positioned in relation to you and how they gesture with the umbrella, their facial expressions, where their eyes dart and when they dart away. Not all talking is verbal – so much so, in fact, that talking need not be verbal at all. Your cocommuter need not have said, 'Please, share my umbrella' in order to have *made known* how they find themselves attuned and *communicated* that to you, while *saying* that the umbrella spoken *about* is a potentially intimate space. They need only have held the umbrella out to you in a certain way.

As Aristotle recognised, the voice (*phōnē*) is one medium through which we, like all animals, communicate pleasure and pain (*Politics* 1253a10;

GA18: 46) and so share how we find ourselves moved by things. But we also communicate this in other ways – not only through our bodily postures and facial expressions but also through our clothing, our overall style, our silences, our musical choices, our culinary habits, and so on. All of these make known to others what matters to us and how things do and can move us. In fact, *all* our modes and manners of engaging with entities express how we find ourselves. This is because all our comporting is a matter of responding to solicitings and so reflects how things matter to us, and because all our comporting is talking and so makes known and communicates (more or less explicitly, more or less precisely, and more or less successfully) to others. Everything that we do talks. And, as we have seen, our talking affects others.

It follows that we are all constantly talking with one another and sharing how we find ourselves, giving uptake to how others find themselves, and developing shared attunements out of this dynamic. This is presumably how public moods arise – from fashions and fads to the cultural climate or the *Zeitgeist*. They express a shared sense of what matters (drought! public transit! 1960s British rock!) and how things are going (not bad! to hell in a handbasket!). I think this is what Heidegger means, despite his agential language, when he says that *das Man* 'has in general its own way of being attuned [*Gestimmtheit*]' and also 'needs attunements and "makes" them for itself' (SZ: 138). These public moods are both particular attunings to specific entities and situations (such as fear of drought) as well as general affective tonalities that provide context for and shape individual affective experiences (such as a general cultural anxiety about the future). Insofar as we are members of the relevant community and share a way of talking with – and so are in conversation with – other members of that community, we will be attuned by the public mood and attuned to situations as that mood disposes us.

It is 'in such a mood and out of such a mood that the orator speaks. He must understand the possibilities of moods in order to rouse them and guide them aright' (SZ: 138–9; GA18: 170). The orator is that speaker who talks in order to manipulate the mood of the crowd. (Aristotle considers how the orator does this in his *Rhetoric*, which is accordingly both an exploration of *pathē* and 'the first systematic hermeneutic of the everydayness of being with one another' (SZ: 138; cf. Agosta, 2010).) The orator brings the crowd into a shared attunement – particularly, fear (*Rhet.* 1382a21ff.; GA20: 394) and anger (*Rhet.* 1380a2–4), but perhaps also hope – through their tone and body language and by speaking of, and so orienting the crowd toward, some entity or entities that are fearsome, unjust, or hopeful. But they do this in such a way that they do not merely direct the audience toward how some particular entities matter. The successful orator brings the audience into a whole field of possible solicitings, in which they are globally attuned – fearfully, angrily, hopefully – to certain sorts of matterings. (Think of Tucker Carlson, Barack Obama.) Their talk shapes the audience's entire disposition, gifting them a whole world of mattering or what we might call 'a frame of mind'. By shaping not just how entities show up but the entire context of ways in which things can matter, the orator shapes the world.

In his later work, Heidegger calls the orator who thus creates worlds 'the poet'. He has Hölderlin in mind (GA39: 146; GA4 *passim*) but we might add Homer, Jesus, Shakespeare, and The Beatles. (In Withy, 2021d, I discuss David Bowie.) In Heidegger's imagination, the poet works alongside the thinker (i.e., Heidegger) and statesperson (i.e., Hitler) (GA39: 144) in order to open up a new historical world for a people. Heidegger writes that 'the poet speaks from out of an attunement' (GA39: 79) and, by bringing the audience into that attunement, 'transport[s them] *out* towards the gods and … *into* the Earth' (GA39: 140), thereby inaugurating a new world. (Compare Heidegger's later notion of the world as the fourfold).

Heidegger reserved a special role for poetry and attunements even in his early work, where he writes that talk can become poetic and so creative: 'In "poetical" discourse, the communication of existential possibilities of *Befindlichkeit* can become an aim in itself, and this amounts to a disclosing of existence' (SZ: 162). Heidegger puts the point more explicitly in *History of the Concept of Time*: "The disclosedness of Dasein, in particular the *Befindlichkeit* of Dasein, can be made manifest by means of words in such a way that certain new possibilities of Dasein's being are set free. Thus talk, especially *poetry*, can even bring about the release of new possibilities of the being of Dasein' (GA20: 375). That is, through talking we can not only share attunements but also generate new possibilities for attunement – new configurations of mattering, new ways of finding ourselves situated, new ways of being-in-the-world with others.

I cannot here give a full account of how poetising makes new attunements and worlds possible, since it requires a deeper dive into talking and poetising than is appropriate. (For a start on the account, see Withy (2021d) and for more on attunements that are grounding, see Section 3.4.) Let me end on two related points. First, the work that poetising does in inaugurating new worlds is driven by the fact that talking is connected with finding. That the speaker's mode of finding is shared, and that the hearer is brought into that attunement, is more important to how poetry works, in this regard, than the fact that it says things about entities (GA39: 14). So, more important than any propositional content is the fact that 'the poet speaks from out of an attunement, an attunement that determines and attunes [*be-stimmt*] the ground and soil that permeates [*durchstimmt*] the space upon which and within which the poetic telling founds a way of being' (GA39: 79). This passage brings us to a second point: in his later work, Heidegger thinks of worlds less as opened up by our taking up projects in understanding, as he does in *Being and Time*, and more as coming to join communities united by shared attunements inaugurated by powerful orators. Talking, being-with, and *Befindlichkeit* together come to new prominence in the account of what it is to be in the world.

—

Heidegger's account of *Befindlichkeit* cannot be understood in isolation from his accounts of being-with, talking, understanding, mattering, and meaning. Together, these make up a unified picture of what it is to be as being-in-the-world. *Befindlichkeit* is that part of the account that captures the fact that, and explains how, we can be affected by things. We are affected by things that are meaningful in the context of the pursuits that we take up. Since we take up those pursuits with others, others are affected along with us – and they are also among the things that can affect us. What affects us or moves us is what matters to us and what matters to us does so because it has been brought back to our thrown being in such a way that it puts our pursuits at stake. We stake ourselves on our encounters with entities and this is what allows us to find ourselves amidst them and able to be touched by them. To be finding is to be profoundly vulnerable and exposed to entities.

Indeed, '[i]n attunement there occurs the inaugural exposure to entities' (GA39: 143). We encounter entities first of all not as inert objects but as mattering to us and moving us. In the next section, I consider some of the ways in which things can so move us, by considering the *Stimmungen* in which they do so.

3 *Stimmungen*

Stimmungen or attunements are the ways in which our being finding expresses itself in the course of our lives. Since *Befindlichkeit* or finding accounts for the fact that things can get to us, *Stimmungen* are affective phenomena, broadly construed. Heidegger says that they 'have long been well-known ontically under the terms "affects" [*Affekte*] and "feelings" [*Gefühle*]' (SZ: 138). He also suggests that sensation might be a mode of *Befindlichkeit* (SZ: 137), which is plausible given that the senses are paradigmatic ways in which we are touched (as it were) by things. I have suggested elsewhere that entities can matter to us in sensation insofar as we pursue the project of embodied existing and allow how things feel, taste, smell, sound, and look to put that project at stake (Withy, 2019: 173). I also argue there that being normatively responsive is a mode of finding (171–2), since it is a way of being open to matterings – to what is required, prohibited, polite, and so on – that arises when we stake the success of our projects on rules or expectations. (This is what the scofflaw does not do, and it would imply that *Befindlichkeit* is that part of our unified disclosing in which we find the origin of normativity.) We can work backwards from other types of mattering to other ways of being open to them, and so to further classes of *Stimmungen*. Other types of mattering that remain to be accommodated include that in religious experience (in which we are attuned to the sacred and profane), that in moral intuition (in which we are attuned to the morally right and wrong), and that in aesthetic experience (in which we are attuned to the beautiful and the plain).

Most intriguing, at least to me, is being-in-the-weather as a potential mode of *Befindlichkeit*. The weather is a literal 'atmosphere in which we first immerse ourselves in each case and which then attunes us through and through' (GA29/ 30: 100). Weather events such as rain are paradigm cases of entities that put us at stake and determine how things (including, but not only, umbrellas) can and do matter to us. We are deeply attuned not only to the weather but also to the climate and the seasons and this attuning determines and is determined both by our embodiment (since it is as embodied that we are weather-experiencing) and by our being-with-others (since the weather is the most fundamental context in which our shared lives play out; this is why much 'small talk' is about the weather). Being-in-the-weather thus strikes me as a plausible and primary way in which we find ourselves attuned to matterings – at least as significant as, if less philosophically familiar than, being in a mood.

But it is being in a mood that captures Heidegger's imagination. In this section, I explore what it is to be in a mood (Section 3.1) and consider the moods that Heidegger spends the most time discussing: fear (Section 3.1), angst (Section 3.2), and boredom (Section 3.3). These *Stimmungen* are to be understood not as qualitatively distinct inner experiences but as different ways in which things can get to us. Among *Stimmungen*, some are special because what gets to us in them is nothing ontic but something ontological. I conclude by considering these ground-attunements (Section 3.4) and also what it is to be authentically attuned (Section 3.5).

3.1 Being in a Mood

We are always attuned in some way – which is to say, we always find ourselves thrown into some situation, encountered by things that matter to us. '[I]n all of what we do and where we dwell, we are in some sense – as we say – "affected" [*zumute*]' (GA20: 352); 'Dasein is always attuned [*gestimmt ist*]' (SZ: 134). If the category of *Stimmungen* includes phenomena such as sensing and being normatively responsive, then this is hardly a controversial claim. But Heidegger seems to mean by it that we are always in some mood. This leads him to give an account of our ordinary, everyday being in a mood.

While we tend to think of moods as 'powerful forces that permeate and envelop us', 'com[ing] over us and things together with one fell swoop' (GA39: 89), most everyday moods will be more subtle:

> At first and for the most part we are affected only by particular attunements that tend toward 'extremes', like joy or grief. A faint apprehensiveness or a buoyant contentment are less noticeable. Apparently not there at all, and yet there, is precisely that *lack of attunement* [*Ungestimmtheit*] in which we are neither out of sorts nor in a 'good' mood. Yet even in this 'neither/nor' we are never without an attunement. (GA29/30: 102; cf. GA18: 51, GA39: 142)

Our everyday apparent lack of mood is a 'sense of sameness, dreariness, emptiness, and staleness' (GA20: 352). It might take the form of the 'undisturbed equanimity' or 'the inhibited ill-humour of our everyday concern' (SZ: 134), but in either case it is 'the pallid lack of attunement [*Ungestimmtheit*] which dominates the "grey everyday" through and through' (SZ: 345; cf. SZ: 134). Heidegger calls it 'indifference' [*Gleichgültigkeit*] (SZ: 345). It is not a true lack of mood but a condition in which 'Dasein becomes satiated with itself' (SZ: 134). 'Satiated' implies that needs are met, desires fulfilled. For us as finding, this means: entities do not really put my pursuits at stake; I am not really vulnerable to them, for good or for ill; they will be there (more or less) when I need them but will not profoundly help or hinder me (cf. Section 2.2). Such a way of finding oneself thrown veers toward inauthenticity since it very nearly denies that one is thrown into and depends on entities other than oneself. But it could also be the everyday indifference of taking things for granted and being more or less comfortable and so satisfied. This is plausibly the mood of our modern, everyday going-about-our-lives.

Such everyday indifference is not entirely unlike the theoretical gaze, which also purports to be unmoved by things and so to be unmooded. The theoretical gaze pretends to see the entities that it studies as present-at-hand objects, shorn of all mattering. 'Yet even the purest *theōria* has not left all attunement behind it; even when we look theoretically at what is just present-at-hand, it does not show itself purely as it looks unless this *theōria* lets it come towards us in a tranquil tarrying alongside' (SZ: 138). This mood of tranquil tarrying allows entities to show up as mattering in terms of our observational project – and 'nothing else is able to address me but the matter being researched' (GA89: 252). This is a highly disciplined – and likely hard-won – way of being attuned and (although Heidegger does not note this) it makes it possible for the other moods and emotions of scientific investigation to emerge: the elation of discovery, the frustration of failure, the perplexity that drives inquiry. Theoretical inquiry can be highly emotional. Even when it is not, it is always mooded.

From the fact that we are always in some mood it follows that the transition *out of* some mood is always a transition *into* some other mood (SZ: 136; GA39: 142). 'There is only ever a change of attunement' (GA29/30: 102). As we have seen, we come into new attunements when we encounter new entities – whether ready-to-hand entities or other people – that shift our disposition. Heidegger also allows that we can 'master' this transition and become 'masters' of our attunements (SZ: 136). His point, in context, is that this is the only case in which volition and cognition have any priority over attunement; ordinarily, willing and thinking are secondary to our finding ourselves situated amidst entities that matter (see Section 4.2). The case in which we can control our attunement at will and through thinking is presumably the one in which we decide to talk ourselves out of or into attunements, just as others talk us into attunements (see Section 2.5): *Look, the rain is clearing! No need to fear.*[11] Even when we 'master a mood' in this way, we never surrender our being attuned: 'we do so by way of a counter-attunement [*Gegenstimmung*]; we are never free of attunement' (SZ: 136).

In addition to tranquil tarrying alongside the present-at-hand and everyday indifference, Heidegger mentions attunements and ground-attunements (see Section 3.4) including: equanimity (SZ: 134, 345; GA9: 311), reticence (GA20: 369), 'enthusiasm, gaiety' (SZ: 345), 'satiety, sadness, melancholy, and desperation' (SZ: 345), 'contentment, bliss, sadness, melancholy, anger' (GA29/30: 96), 'sadness, cheerfulness, boringness' (GA29/30: 127), and 'even the coldness of calculation, even the prosaic sobriety of planning are traits of an attunement [*Gestimmtheit*]' (GA11: 24–5). (There are surely others.) Brief mentions of joy (*Freude*) can be found (e.g., SZ: 310, 345; GA18: 198; GA29/30: 96; GA71: 99, 172) along with tantalising definitions: it is 'a specific lightness of being-in-the-world' (GA18: 48; cf. GA18: 59–60); it is taken 'in the presence of the Dasein . . . of a human being whom we love' (GA9: 110); it is the 'counter-attunement' (*Gegenstimmung*) to holy mourning (GA39: 145) (see also GA71: 217, 219; GA39: 148). So too for hope (SZ: 345; GA18: 260; GA60: 102, 151, 297) and respect (qua Kant's '"susceptibility" to the moral law', one's 'subordinating' or 'submitting' oneself to it (GA3: 156f.)). Heidegger discusses at somewhat greater length attunements including wonder, shock, and holy mourning (see Section 3.4). The moods he dwells on most are angst (*Angst*) (see Section 3.2), boredom (*Langeweile*) (see Section 3.3), and fear (*Furcht*).

---

[11] McManus (2019: 144) offers a different interpretation: we master our moods when we suppress the full range of how things matter to us in order to accord with 'a generally-accepted and exculpatory public sentiment about "how one must act"'. That is: we master our moods by submitting to *das Man*'s sense of how we should feel.

Fear is Heidegger's standard example of a *Stimmung*, used to demonstrate the structure of *Stimmungen* and how they are modes of *Befindlichkeit* (SZ: §30; GA20: §30a; Withy (2021a)). Any *Stimmung* will manifest the three essential characteristics of *Befindlichkeit*: disclosing us as thrown, opening a world of possible solicitings and disclosing the whole of being-in-the-world, and allowing entities to matter to and move us.

The entities that get to us in fearing are entities (including events) that threaten our pursuits in one way or another: perishing or demise, the climate crisis, rain while we wait for the bus to work, damage to our books, and so on. Some such threatening and menacing entity is that in-the-face-of-which (*das Wover*) we fear (SZ: 140; GA20: 395). It threatens when it 'is not yet within striking distance, but it is coming close' (SZ: 140) not necessarily in space but as a live risk to our pursuits (Withy, 2022a: 310–13, 2019: 166). (Can we fear ourselves (Blattner, 1999: 48 n. 27)? This is an interesting question; it amounts to asking whether we can genuinely threaten to torpedo the projects that we are earnestly pursuing.) In discovering the repelling entity, fearing also discloses us to ourselves – as threatened and put at risk. It is we ourselves, in our pursuits, about which we fear: '*That which* fear fears *about* [*das Worum*] is that very entity which is afraid – Dasein. . . . Fearing discloses this entity as endangered and abandoned to itself' (SZ: 141; cf. GA30: 396–7). We are revealed as stuck with our vulnerable selves and projects, and as stuck with the threatening situation that we are in.

We might object that sometimes we fear not about ourselves but about entities (*My books will get wet!*) or other people (*What if my friend is crushed by their grief?*). Heidegger holds that these are indirect ways of fearing for ourselves (SZ: 142; Blattner, 1999: 49–50) – for our own project of being a bibliophile, or our own pursuit of a friendship with our grieving friend. In the latter sort of case, 'what one "is apprehensive about" is one's being-with with the other, who might be torn away from one' (SZ: 142). I disagree with Heidegger that fearing for others is really fearing for ourselves. He needs to better appreciate how, in the case of those whom we care about, we take on board that which can move them and allow that to move us – as we promise to do, for instance, in a marriage vow (Withy, 2022a). Working this out fully requires working out how we take up shared pursuits with others and so open shared worlds of mattering and meaning.

Opening a world of fearful matterings is the remaining structural moment of fear. As we saw earlier, this fearfulness (*Furchtsamkeit*) is part of our affective repertoire and is what first allows us to encounter entities in terms of threats, safe havens, sources of protection, and so on. We open this range of possible ways in which things can matter by bringing entities back to our own thrown being and first allowing them to put our pursuits at stake (see Section 2.2). This is our submitting to the world and it discloses our entire being-in-the-world as existing, finding, and falling (see Section 2.4). (Some interpreters align this moment of fear with the *mood* of fear and the other two structural moments with fear as an *emotion* (e.g., Elpidorou & Freeman, 2015: 668; Ratcliffe, 2009: 358–9) but this not only mistakes the phenomenology of being in a mood, it misses the point of Heidegger's analysis, which is to explain how things can get to us rather than to track the folk-psychological distinction between mood and emotion.)

There are various modifications of fear, based on different ways in which we can be threatened (GA20: 397–8; SZ: 121). But Heidegger is not concerned to explore these distinctions. He is not interested in better understanding fear as an emotion or a mood. He is interested in how fear discloses our being, discloses the world, and allows entities to matter to us. This is the basic structure of fear as a disclosive attunement: it (i) discovers some entity, in the face of which we fear (*das Wovor*, the in-the-face-of-which); (ii) discloses ourselves, as that about which we fear (*das Worum*, the about-which); (iii) discloses the world as a context of potential matterings within which entities threaten us, which is our fearfulness. This tripartite structure can be used to analyse any attunement. (Compare Aristotle's concept of the mean in the *Nicomachean Ethics*, which shows that each pathos has a how, when, whither, and about which [*das Wie, Wann, Wozu und Worüber*] (GA18: 171; *Eth. Nic.* 1106b21–3).) By seeing how angst fills out this structure differently, we can see how it discloses differently from fear. In angst, something threatening gets to us. But what gets to us is not an entity.

3.2 Angst

Heidegger analyses angst (*Angst*, anxiety, dread) in *History of the Concept of Time* (GA20: §30), *Being and Time* (SZ: §40), and 'What Is Metaphysics?' (in GA9), and he does so because it discloses in a 'distinctive' and 'far-reaching' way (SZ: 139) (Withy, 2021a). Its disclosing is distinctive insofar as it has no ontic content, reaching instead all the way to ontological structures. We saw that fear is (i) in the face of some entity which it discovers, (ii) about ourselves, who are disclosed, and (iii) world-disclosing, which is the attuning itself (fearfulness). In angst, entities are discovered as mattering – but in the mode of insignificance. The world is disclosed – but in its very character as world. And our Dasein is revealed, in its very being as being-in-the-world. As Heidegger interprets each of these, they amount to the claims that angst (i) is anxious in the face of no particular entity but instead our being-in-the-world, (ii) is about no particular aspect of our lives but instead our very being-in-the-world, and (iii) is the attuning that is itself being-in-the-world. The three structural moments of angst's disclosing coincide:

they are all being-in-the-world (SZ: 188). So, whereas in an attunement such as fear our pursuits are threatened by some entity in the world that gets to us and moves us, in angst our very being as being-in-the-world gets to us. Angst is an ontological self-affection (cf. Shockey, 2016: 22): an autopathos and an ontopathos.

I begin with (ii), that which angst is anxious about. 'Angst is anxious about naked Dasein as something that has been thrown into uncanniness. It brings back' not to any particular pursuit that we have taken up and are now stuck with but 'to the pure "that-it-is" of one's ownmost individualised thrownness' (SZ: 343). As we saw, this 'that it is' is a burden: the burden of having to be as one is and going on with one's pursuits. This burden is manifest in all attunements as our being stuck with the situation that we are in and having to play the hand that we are dealt. But whereas in ordinary attunements it is the burden of *this* situation and *this* particular hand, in angst it is the burden of having to play any hand at all. This is a distinctive kind of burden because it is not something that we can readily make intelligible. I find myself playing this game (as it were) of being Dasein, but how did I end up here, with this responsibility? I did not ask to be a case of Dasein, I did not choose it, and there is no intelligible causal chain that accounts for the fact that I have to live out my life as a case of Dasein (since causal chains account for other sorts of facts). Why do I have to do this? I just do. The fact of this is a burden and its inexplicability is a threat to our most fundamental pursuit: sense-making (Withy, 2014). Heidegger calls this threat 'uncanniness' (*Unheimlichkeit*) (SZ: 189; GA20: 402) and says that it 'pursues Dasein constantly' (SZ: 189) (see Withy, 2015a). In angst, we face up to this threat *in* and *to* our being-in-the-world.

As in Søren Kierkegaard's (1981 (1844)) account of angst, what threatens is not some entity but instead possibility.[12] Our 'being-possible' is our possibility of pursuing some project or another. *Which* project we each pursue or continue to pursue is open but *that* we must each pursue some project(s) is a necessity of our being. This necessity and its corresponding responsibility falls on each of us, for each of us to take up in our lives. In angst, this responsibility of possibility, which we have by virtue of our being, is manifest: 'with that which it is anxious about, angst discloses Dasein as *being-possible*, and indeed as the only kind of thing which it can be of its own accord as something individualized in individualization' (SZ: 187–8). This is the individualised responsibility that

---

[12] Heidegger acknowledges (and criticises as too psychological) Kierkegaard's account of angst (GA20: 404; SZ: 190niv). For Heidegger's debt to Kierkegaard, see Kisiel (1993: 550n9), Dreyfus (1991: 283–340), and Carlisle (2015). As Kisiel reminds us: 'The purportedly Kierkegaardian concepts of *Angst* (SZ190b) and *Existenz* (SZ235b) ... [come to Heidegger] by way of at least Paul, Augustine, Aristotle, and Jaspers' (Kisiel, 1993: 550n9). Heidegger holds that angst was 'glimpsed' by Augustine and Luther (GA20: 404; SZ: 190n4) and that even Aristotle had an intimation of it (GA18: 192).

authentic cases of Dasein take up and from which inauthentic cases of Dasein flee.

But it is not just our being-possible that threatens; it is also the possibility of the world as a field of affordings or meanings. In a sense, these are one and the same burdensome possibility, since taking up a pursuit is what opens up the world as a space of possibilities. In angst, '[t]he *possibility* of the ready-to-hand in general' 'oppresses us [*ist was beengt*]' (SZ: 187). This is because the world in its worldhood – as a network of possible ways in which entities can afford and so be meaningful – has become obtrusive and is 'oppressively present in an obtrusiveness' (GA20: 401). Heidegger here uses language that he also uses when he analyses how the breakdown of tools reveals the world (SZ: §16; GA20: §23a). He says that the world as revealed in angst is obtrusive (*aufdringlich*) (SZ: 187; GA20: 401) and obstinate (*aufsässig*) (SZ: 186). It is not said to be conspicuous and so is not analogous to a broken tool (cf. SZ: 73). Instead, this breakdown is analogous to when some tool is missing and other entities stand out obtrusively (SZ: 73) and when some tool obstinately gets in the way of our activity (SZ: 74). So, the claim is that the world is salient and in the way and that it is so because something necessary is absent.

What is absent or suspended is our projecting ourselves forward onto concrete pursuits. (Compare Haugeland's (2000: 63) suggestion that Heidegger's 'anxiety is analogous to [Thomas] Kuhn's sense of crisis', in which someone previously committed to the day-to-day pursuit of a science finds themselves unable to go on with it.) In angst, we 'find[] nothing in terms of which [we] might be able to understand' ourselves (SZ: 343). Precisely how and why this occurs is one of two (related) foci in the debate about how to interpret Heidegger's angst.[13]

However we understand it, our suspended projecting must leave intact the world as a field of possible affordings so that it can show up and impress itself upon us. This obstinacy of the world is what, in turn, prevents us from taking it as a background to the foreground of our dealings with entities that mean and matter. Normally, we just engage with entities by responding to their offers of affording. We wait for the bus, for example. But in angst we are, as it were, impressed by the fact that *bus stops are places where we wait for the bus* – and *buses are public means of transiting between places* – and indeed (*etc. etc.*) *the whole world is a network of such affordings*. When we tune into the very fact of such affordings, we cannot hear that or what they are offering us by way of

---

[13] To mention just one of the many interpretations: Blattner's (1994) reading has the significant virtue of explaining how and why angst is said to *be* being-towards-death (SZ: 266) and *in the face of* death (SZ: 251, 254, 265–6) since Blattner identifies angst's breakdown of projects with death's impossibility of being Dasein.

possibilities for engaging. Our comporting toward entities thus also breaks down: angst 'brings Dasein back from its falling absorption in the "world"' (SZ: 189) and entities show up as 'insignificant' (*Unbedeutsamkeit*) (SZ: 187), 'not "relevant" [*relevant*] at all' (SZ: 186).

Precisely in what sense entities are insignificant is the second focus of debate in how we interpret angst (and one's interpretation of it governs how one presents the phenomenology of angst as an experience). 'Significance' (*Bedeutsamkeit*) is a technical term in *Being and Time* and it refers to the meanings or affordings that things as a whole have by virtue of their being coordinated with our pursuits (SZ: 87). In angst, then, entities 'no longer have any affordance [*Bewandtnis*]' (SZ: 343). What does this mean? On one reading, to lack significance is for things to show up as bereft of – and so, beyond or exceeding – any meaning that they might have by virtue of that coordination (e.g., Käufer, 2005: 487) (for the notion of the excess in entities beyond meaning, see Polt (2011); for a rebuttal, see Withy (2022b: §5)). Entities show up in their brute thereness – and perhaps even in their mere materiality, as in Jean-Paul Sartre's (2007 (1938)) nausea (Ratcliffe, 2008: 356, 2009: 71). We experience entities as unmeaning and radically other.

Another reading takes entities to retain the meaning that they inherit from our pursuits but holds that that affording becomes inert and incapable of becoming any form of soliciting because our projecting on our pursuits has been suspended (e.g., Blattner, 2006: 140–1; Dreyfus, 1991: 179; Withy, 2015a: 56–7). That suspension divorces the affording of things from us and introduces distance between us and the meanings of things. On this sort of interpretation, when we are angst-ridden we experience entities as meaningful but irrelevant (as in phenomena such as depersonalisation/derealisation (Withy, 2015a: 58) and depression (Blattner, 2006: 142)).[14]

So far, entities are insignificant and we are not pursuing any projects. As a result, the world as space of possible affordings stands out. This is what oppresses us in angst: 'What oppresses us is not this or that, nor is it the summation of everything present-at-hand; it is rather the *possibility* of the ready-to-hand in general; that is to say, it is the world itself' (SZ: 187). Thus (i) 'the world as such is that in the face of which one has angst [*das Wovor der Angst ist die Welt als solche*]' (SZ: 187, original italicised), as opposed to some

---

[14] There are other interpretations of the type of breakdown involved in angst that do not fit neatly into these categories. See, e.g., Magid (2016: 451–2) and McManus (2015). McManus (2015: 166) frames the question of the sort of breakdown involved in angst in terms of the problem of how we return to our pursuit-driven lives after experiencing angst ('the Motivation Problem'). On that problem, see also Golob (2017).

particular entity, as in fear. No entity gets to us in angst; the world (*kosmos*) does. Angst is a kosmopathos.

But this kosmopathos is, in the end, a self-affection or autopathos. For the world is a component of being-in-the-world. It is a field of possibilities opened up by our projecting on some possible pursuit and it is what it is only insofar as we dwell in it and allow entities to be meaningful and to matter on the basis of it. It is the burden, necessity, and threat of this – of having to be as being-in-the-world – that makes angst anxious in the face of the world.

We have seen that (ii) in angst we are anxious *about* our being-in-the-world and (i) *in the face of* the world as a component of being-in-the-world. These two structural moments of angst coincide (SZ: 342–3; GA20: 402, 405). So, in fact, does the third: (iii) the being-attuned of angst is being-in-the-world (SZ: 188). This is to say, at the very least, that angst is the fundamental tenor and tone of being-in-the-world: 'angst is nothing other than the pure and simple experience of being in the sense of being-in-the-world' (GA20: 403). Heidegger inherits this view of the human condition from early Christianity (Kisiel, 1993: 114, 182–3; Withy, 2021a) and especially from Augustine, who views the earthly human condition as fundamentally restless and eager to return to God (*Confessions* 1.1 *et passim*).[15] On Earth, we are unhomely. To cope, we either distract ourselves with worldly pursuits – in Augustine's case, seeking recognition and power and falling prey to various lusts – or we turn away from the world and toward our inner connection to the divine. So, too, in Heidegger: we deal with the fundamental angst of being-in-the-world by either inauthentically fleeing into the public world (SZ: 188–9; GA20: 405) or authentically facing up to our being.

So understood, angst is the ground of both authenticity (Section 3.5) and falling qua inauthentic immersion in *das Man*. There is also a sense in which angst is the ground of falling qua being-absorbed in entities (SZ: 184, 186; GA3: 238; GA9: 114f.; GA20: 392ff., 403). Dreyfus (1991: 313) argues that Heidegger's claim that angst grounds falling is his 'secularizing … [of] Kierkegaard's interpretation of the Christian doctrine of the fall' and that this secularisation introduces a motivational element into falling as an existentiale. We live out our lives amidst entities not simply because that is what it is to be us but because we are fleeing the angst in our being in order to repress or conceal it.

---

[15] Scheler (2010: 143) takes Heidegger's focus on angst to reveal less about the human condition per se and more about the influence of Christianity (including Protestantism) on the West. He raises a question that many other readers also raise: Could not hope – or, we might add, wonder or joy – have been the ground-attunement of the human condition? For more on Scheler's criticisms of Heidegger on angst and care, see Dahlstrom (2002).

This makes falling qua absorption similar to falling qua inauthenticity and contributes to Heidegger's persistent conflating of the two.

Heidegger avoids this problem in 'What Is Metaphysics?' (1929) by removing the idea that it is *we* who flee what is disclosed in angst. He characterises what is revealed in angst as inherently repelling. As in *Being and Time*, angst is in the face of no particular thing and so in the face of nothing (SZ: 186; GA9: 111). But where 'the nothing' in the face of which we are anxious in *Being and Time* is 'the most primordial something' (SZ: 187) – namely, the world as a context of possible affordings and solicitings –in 'What Is Metaphysics?' the nothing is the counterconcept to entities as a whole.[16] (*Pace* Stephan Käufer (2005), who reads the two accounts as consistent on the referent of 'the nothing'. Richard Polt (2001: 67–8) writes of 'the nothing' that 'Heidegger uses the expression tactically rather than strategically: it serves various functions for him in various contexts throughout his philosophical career.') The nothing in 'What Is Metaphysics?' is the phenomenon of emptiness that we approach when we wonder why there are entities at all *rather than nothing*. This empty other-than-entities is revealed in angst and it is 'essentially repelling' (GA9: 114) and 'directs us precisely towards entities' (GA9: 116). The repelling push toward entities is the proper activity of the nothing (*das Nichts*): its nihilating or noth-ing (*nichtet*) (GA9: 114).[17] Such falling toward entities is not a motivated flight from angst but is built into being-in-the-world.

So, the claim is that '[i]n the clear night of the nothing of angst the original openness of entities as such arises: that they are entities – and not nothing' (GA9: 114). Our absorbed falling and being-amidst entities is grounded in an original, anxious exposure to the nothing. But that anxious exposure must then lie at the ground of our being, not as a mood or an experienced affect but as an inaugural openness. It must be 'the fundamental occurrence of our Dasein' (GA9: 110) – what I have elsewhere called 'originary angst' (Withy, 2015a:

---

[16] Rudolf Carnap (1931) critcised Heidegger for his talk of 'the nothing' in 'What Is Metaphysics?', claiming that 'nothing' is meaningless when used as a substantive. Heidegger scholars agree that Carnap misunderstands how Heidegger deploys the term and neglects Heidegger's broader and reasonable departures from and criticisms of Carnap's basic philosophical assumptions (e.g., Polt, 2001; Käufer, 2005, 2001: 472; Ratcliffe, 2002: 294, 2008: 58ff.).

[17] Heidegger plausibly has the idea of an angst or fear that can push us to flee *toward*, rather than cause us to flee *from*, from Augustine, who distinguishes *timor servilis* (servile fear), which is worldly fear, from *timor castus* (pure fear), which is selfly fear (GA60: §7; GA18: 178; GA20: 404; Withy 2021a). Worldly fear corresponds to Heidegger's fear, since both aim to repel a worldly threat and to flee from it. Selfly fear anticipates Heidegger's angst (Kisiel, 1993: 214–16, 490) and 'does not have the direction of keeping something or someone at bay, but of pulling something or someone toward oneself' (GA60: 297). One significant difference is that Augustine's *timor castus* is a flight toward the good (God) while Heidegger's encounter with the nothing in angst pushes us to flee toward innerworldly entities. Insofar as such angst exposes us to our being, however, it can be viewed as a movement toward our authentic selves.

ch. 2). Thus Heidegger says that 'the essence of angst is Dasein itself' (GA20: 405), that angst is 'constitutive of the being of Dasein *qua* care' (GA20: 391), and that it 'belongs to Dasein's essential state [*wesenhaften Daseinsverfassung*] of being-in-the-world' (SZ: 189). If this angst is not a mood that we experience, it must be some sort of ontological attunement – and a condition of other attunements: 'an event which underlies all instances of finding oneself in the midst of entities which already are' (GA3: 238) and which 'makes possible in advance the manifestness of entities in general' (GA9: 114). (Apparently, even the ancient Greeks understood this: 'For the Greeks, fear as angst is co-constitutive of the manner and mode of grasping what is and what is not' (GA18: 192).)

Such originary angst is 'usually repressed' (GA9: 117), implicit (GA20: 404), concealed (GA9: 118), or latent (SZ: 189) in the sense that it is not a part of our being that we usually experience. But we do experience it sometimes, in the mood of angst. The experienced attunement of angst tunes us into the anxious attuning at the ground of our being, revealing to us our original opening onto the nothing and its nihilating push toward entities. What this mood of angst looks like in experience and how often it occurs, I do not know. But in opening us to the originary angst at the ground of our being, it opens us to our being at its ground. It is a profound self-disclosure; an autopathos.[18]

So when Heidegger says that (iii) the attuning of angst is being-in-the-world, he means either (or both) that the fundamental tonality of our being is anxious or (/and) that an originary angst attunes us at our ground and is our foundational openness to entities (or something in between). In either case, such angst is analogous to the disposition of fearfulness, which opens a world of possible ways in which things can matter. Similarly, originary angst is a ground-attunement that opens up being-in-the-world as a space within which self, world, and entities can be intelligible. And it has a threatening, uncanny, and angsty character for us, as sense-makers, because 'it is quite incomprehensible' why we must be in the world – why we must play this risky game of being a self, in the world, amidst entities – at all: 'why entities are to be *uncovered*, why *truth* and *Dasein* must be' (SZ: 228).

Originary angst is an attunement *at* the ground of our being; it is itself the origin or ground. And as the mood in which we are opened to that origin or ground, the mood of angst is an attunement *of* the ground. As an attunement of and at the ground, angst is a ground-attunement (*Grundstimmung*) (GA9: 111, 112) or ground-finding (*Grundbefindlichkeit*) (SZ: 342; GA3: 237; GA20: 391). In order

---

[18]   I argue that originary angst is also an autopathos – and further, a self-finding that, in finding itself, makes itself possible – in Withy (2015a: ch. 2).

to better illuminate what a ground-attunement is (Section 3.4), let me consider the only ground-attunement that Heidegger discusses at length: boredom.

3.3 Boredom

When Heidegger analyses the ground-attunement of boredom in his lecture course *The Fundamental Concepts of Metaphysics: World, Finitude, Solitude* (1929–30), he abandons the tripartite structure that he used earlier to analyse fear and angst and instead considers three different 'levels' or 'depths' of boredom. At each depth lies a deeper form of ontopathos, which suggests that Heidegger's goal is not so much to illuminate what happens when people feel bored but to explore what it is for (our) being to affect us. While the ground-attunement of angst is a kosmopathos, in which the world oppresses us, in boredom what oppresses us is time: '[i]n boredom [*Langeweile*], the while [*Weile*] becomes long [*lang*]' (GA29/30: 228). Time – the time that we are – gets to us. So boredom is a chronopathos: 'becoming bored is a being affected by time' (GA29/30: 148).

At each depth of boredom, time bores us (GA29/30: 236) in a different way. In the first form of boredom, we are bored by some particular thing, person, or place (GA29/30: 124), such as the train station in which we are waiting for a train (GA29/30: 140). Nothing engages us and time drags on. In the second form of boredom, the time does not drag on but passes us by, abandoning us to ourselves, as when we pass a perfectly pleasant evening at a dinner party but find that the whole evening leaves us empty (GA29/30: 180). In the third form – profound boredom – we are brought up out of any particular situation and away from ourselves as the specific people that we are. With our lives and comporting suspended, we confront entities as a whole as indifferent (GA29/30: 207–8) and are exposed to and entranced by the temporality of our own being (GA29/30: 221).

Each form of boredom has two structural moments: (a) being held in limbo (*Hingehaltenheit*) and (b) being left empty (*Leergelassenheit*). That is to say that, in each form of boredom, we are both (a) brought to a stop or stalled and (b) experience an emptiness or void. Both dimensions are readily apparent in the first form of boredom, in which the interval of time between now and when the train will arrive forces us to wait and to fill up the time. When time (a) holds us up and stalls our activity in this way, it (b) stops entities from soliciting us to engage with them. '[B]ecause time refuses *it* something', 'the station refuses *itself*' (GA29/30: 158). Things 'have nothing to offer' (GA29/30: 155) and we pass indifferently from our book to the timetable to the road outside the station with nothing calling out to us. The station and everything in it becomes obtrusive (*aufdringlich*) (GA29/30: 158) because of the way that time oppresses us (*bedrängt uns*) by keeping us waiting and refusing to pass (GA29/30: 144). We watch the seconds slowly tick by.

In the second form of boredom – as exemplified by the dinner party – time does not leave us waiting for it to pass but, since we have set aside the whole evening for the party, time (a) leaves us standing in the span that we have allowed. Over the evening, time 'does not flow – it *stands*' (GA29/30: 295). Heidegger describes this enduring as 'oppressing' (*Bedrängen*) (GA29/30: 184): time 'abandon[s] us' to ourselves and the evening but 'does not release us' from either (GA29/30: 183, original italicised). Having taken time for the evening and so abandoned ourselves to time's enduring, we too are left standing (GA29/30: 210) and (b) left empty by things. It is not that we restlessly seek to be satisfied by things and find them unappealing, as in the first form of boredom, it is that we no longer seek to be satisfied by things at all (GA29/30: 177). We submit to the duration of the evening and allow everything to happen. We are stuck in the evening's enduring, as if in the middle of a stagnant lake.

In profound boredom, we are oppressed by time not as it passes slowly or stands stagnantly but as it expands over and makes up our lives as Dasein (GA29/30: 229). In *Being and Time*, Heidegger had analysed our being as ultimately intelligible temporally, as the unified interplay of the future (of projecting), of the past (of being thrown), and of the present (of comporting toward entities) (SZ: §65). Here, in *The Fundamental Concepts of Metaphysics*, Heidegger also understands us in temporal terms and he understands profound boredom as our being exposed to, and in fact (a) 'entranced by' (GA29/30: 229), the temporality of our being: 'Time entrances Dasein, not as the time which has remained standing as distinct from flowing, but rather the time beyond such flowing and its standing, the time which in each case Dasein itself as a whole is' (GA29/30: 221). Held up by the temporality that we ourselves are in our being, we are also (b) left empty by entities – not the entities that confront us in some situation but entities as a whole. Entities as a whole refuse themselves to us. In other words: we are brought up out of falling. 'Entranced by time, Dasein cannot find its way to those entities that announce themselves in the telling refusal of themselves as a whole' (GA29/30: 221). It 'can no longer bring itself to expect anything from entities as a whole in any respect, because there is not even anything enticing about entities any more. They withdraw as a whole' (GA29/30: 221). (Note that '[i]t is not entities that properly refuse, but time, which itself makes possible the manifestness of these entities as a whole' (GA29/30: 226).) When entities refuse themselves, we are called to our being as Dasein and so to authenticity (GA29/30: 223–4) (see Section 3.5).

Like angst, boredom disrupts falling. It does so because it opens us up to a condition of possibility of our comporting toward entities – namely, time.

Indeed, because all three forms of boredom open us up to time, each disrupts falling in one way or another. In particular, each involves a breakdown of soliciting. (For a different reading, based on a different interpretation of the 'depth' at issue, see (Ratcliffe, 2009: 358, 2013: 164–6).) In the first form of boredom (at the train station), entities remain meaningful but do not call out to us to engage with them; they 'do nothing at all to us, they *leave us completely in peace*' (GA29/30: 154). They 'do not disturb us', '[y]et they do not help us either, they do not take our comportment upon themselves' (GA29/30: 155). The book or the timetable could solicit us to read it but it does not. In the second form of boredom – the dinner party – the breakdown in soliciting is deeper (GA29/30: 210): 'any seeking to be satisfied by entities is absent in advance' (GA29/30: 177). The very possibilities of soliciting have been suspended. Thus, no book could possibly call out to us to read it during the course of the dinner party. Nothing can make demands on us at all, which is why we float through the evening. In profound boredom, soliciting itself becomes impossible because what makes it possible is missing: we do not take up particular projects to which entities could or could not matter. In the absence of our pursuits, entities cannot be brought back to our thrown being and so no world of possible ways of soliciting can open. This is why 'everything indeed, even this being left empty [i.e., the breakdown of soliciting] is indifferent, i.e., impossible. . . . [I]t is boring *for one*; not for me as me, but for one' as an indifferent case of Dasein (GA29/30: 210).

Heidegger puts this breakdown by saying that '[e]ntities have … become indifferent *as a whole* … [and] show themselves precisely as such in their indifference' (GA29/30: 208). But this experience of entities as a whole as indifferent is not an experience of the nothing (GA9: 111; GA29/30: 210). We do not encounter the nothing either as the world (as in angst in *Being and Time*) or the empty *rather than* entities as a whole and as such (as in angst in 'What Is Metaphysics?'). So, boredom cannot ground falling as angst does in 'What Is Metaphysics?'. Nonetheless, like angst, boredom is an attunement *of* the ground, insofar as it opens us to the ground of our being – in this case, our temporal ground. And it is an attunement *at* the ground, insofar as being moved by temporality is what makes for Dasein rather than not, according to *Being and Time*. If to be a case of Dasein is to be moved by time, and if being moved by time is being bored, then our temporal being must be fundamentally bored. (I leave the details of this argument for other interpreters to work out. Among other things, Heidegger's question will need to be answered: 'Is it only in boredom that we are affected by time?' (GA29/30: 148).)

Both boredom and angst are ground-attunements in the same way: they are attunements *of* and *at* the ground of Dasein's being – ontopathē that ground all other possibilities of being affected. I can now give a general account of what it is to be a ground-attunement.

3.4 Ground-Attunements

Angst and boredom are both *Grundstimmungen* (ground-moods, ground-attunements, fundamental or basic attunements) or *Grundbefindlichkeiten* (ground-findings, basic dispositions). (Heidegger uses the terms without apparent differentiation, although he uses the former much more frequently. I will thus speak of *Grundstimmungen*, ground-attunements.) Ground-attunements are distinguished from other attunements by the fact that, in them, we are moved not by entities but by the ontological phenomena that allow us and other entities to be what they are: time, world, the nothing, being, Dasein's being, or the correlation between being and Dasein('s being). (Heidegger will put this by saying that ground-attunements tune us into 'entities as such and as a whole' (GA45: 168), which is to say that they tune us into entities as such, in their *being* – as a whole, and so to *world*.) Because in ground-attunements what get to us are ontological phenomena, 'the attuning intrusion [*stimmenden Einfall*] of the ground-attunement ... [is] radically befalling [*Zu-fall*]' (GA65: 22).

Ground-attunements are attunements *of* the ground in the sense that, in them, we are attuned *by* – moved by, affected by – phenomena at the ground. But further, being open to and affected by such phenomena is what it is to be us. To be a case of Dasein is to be in the world, to be temporal, to be held out into the nothing (GA9: 115), to be attuned to the call of being (e.g., GA11: 21f.; GA71: 219). Heidegger's account of what is at our ground changes somewhat over time. In particular, as we have seen, in his middle and later periods he emphasises the grounding of the historical community in poetising, for example, over the ground of cases of Dasein, and Dasein as such, in temporality. Precisely *what* is grounded, *in* what, and *how* varies across the course of Heidegger's thought. But *that* we are grounded in our being moved by some grounding phenomenon or phenomena does not change: 'ground-attunement is ... the way in which we are originally transposed into the expanse of entities and the depths of being' (GA39: 142; cf. GA45: 172). So, *at* our ground is our being attuned *to* grounding phenomena in ground-attunements. At our ground, ontological phenomena get to us.

Insofar as they are situated at the ground, ground-attunements are not among the *Stimmungen* that we experience. They belong instead to our being as finding and so to *Befindlichkeit*. Nonetheless, since to be finding is to find ourselves – and to find ourselves *as finding* – ground-attunements can be uncovered in experienced attunements. Even though they are repressed (GA9: 117) or latent

(SZ: 189, 192), they can be evoked; even though they are asleep, they can be awakened (GA29/30: §16). Thus, Heidegger spends the bulk of *The Fundamental Concepts of Metaphysics* attempting to awaken profound boredom (although it is not obvious precisely how he is purporting to do so (see Withy, 2013)).

The reason to awaken and experience a ground-attunement is that it promises ontological insight –specifically, insight into our own being and its openness to being. In *Being and Time*, for example, the analysis of angst is methodologically crucial for the existential analytic (SZ: 182; see also Golob, 2017; Hadjioannou, 2019a; Shockey, 2016; Ward, 2021; Withy, 2012). The reason is that, while the existential analytic aims to illuminate our being, and to do so starting from our everyday going about amidst entities, that everydayness sees us misunderstanding ourselves and distorting the character of our being. To overcome that distortion and misunderstanding, our falling absorption must be disrupted – which is precisely what a ground-attunement does. Further, a ground-attunement does that because it attunes us to our being, which is precisely what the existential analytic is seeking to understand. Thus, 'in angst Dasein gets brought before itself through its own being, so that we can define phenomenologically the character of the entity disclosed in angst, and define it as such in its being' (SZ: 184).

In this way, ground-attunements are crucial methodological tools for Heidegger's phenomenological ontology. Indeed, since any theorising or thinking has its attunement (see Section 3.1), philosophising will always be in some mood. Better if that mood is one that opens us to a ground-attunement and so provides ontological insight! We must in every case 'attune our questioning attitude to the right ground-attunement or, to put it more prudently, allow the ground-attunement a first resonance' (GA45: 1). This position raises the question of what it is for our questioning to be mooded or attuned to a ground-attunement such as angst. R. Matthew Shockey (2016), for example, provocatively argues that the angst that Heidegger has in mind is an ontological affect with no felt component and that, at most, we must imagine – not experience – a mood of existential breakdown in order to philosophise. But while Heidegger is clear that imagining an attunement is insufficient, at least with regard to boredom (GA29/30: 136), the question remains whether he really intends to hold that we should philosophise while angst-ridden or bored.

Still, it is not particularly radical to suggest that philosophising takes place in a mood. Plato (*Theaetetus* 155d) and Aristotle (*Met.* 982b12) both believed that the origin or *archē* of philosophy is wonder. Heidegger describes wonder (*Erstaunen*) as 'the attunement within which the Greek philosophers were granted the correspondence [*Entsprechen*] to the being of entities'

(GA11: 23). Wonder wonders at entities as a whole as such: it 'brings forth the showing of what is most usual', namely, the fact that entities *are*, 'in its unusualness' (GA45: 168). According to Heidegger, this wondering is history's first opening onto that whole and so the ontological. Thus, wonder is the beginning of the history of ontological and so philosophical questioning – of the Greek philosophical tradition and so of what he calls 'the first inception' (GA11: 22f.; GA45: 155ff. *et passim*; GA65: 15, 46).

We experience something of this beginning in angst, in which entities as a whole 'manifest ... in their full but heretofore concealed strangeness as what is radically other – with respect to nothing' (GA9: 114) and so as worthy of wonder (GA9: 121). (For more on the relationship between angst and wonder, see Balaska, in press.) But Heidegger thinks that we are no longer disposed by the ground-attunement of wonder, since we have moved on from and lost our connection to the original openness of the first, ancient Greek beginning (GA45: 184). Different philosophical eras have different ground-attunements, which tune us into different aspects of our ontological ground, and in different ways: 'the ground-attunement attunes Da-sein and thereby thinking as a projection of the truth of beyng in word and concept' (GA65: 21). Modern philosophy, for example, is attuned not by wonder but by doubt (GA11: 24). For Descartes, 'doubt becomes that attunement [*Stimmung*] in which the attunement [*Gestimmtheit*] ... vibrates to the *ens certum*, i.e., the entity in certainty' (GA11: 24).

Heidegger thinks that our age is philosophically and culturally at the end of the ontological trajectory opened up by the ancient Greeks. In *The Fundamental Concepts of Metaphysics*, he describes contemporary Dasein as deeply bored – so bored, in fact, that what leaves us empty and unmoved is precisely the profound boredom in which we would be opened to our temporality and called to authenticity (see Beistegui, 2000). Being thus closed off from the ground-attunement of profound boredom is not the absence of attunement but the most pressing affliction (*Bedrängnis*) or suffering (pathos): 'what oppresses us most profoundly and in a concealed manner is the very absence of any essential oppressiveness [*Bedrängnis*] in our Dasein as a whole' (GA29/30: 244). This absence *gets to us* in our contemporary boredom. We need to learn to become bored – to be oppressed by time in a chronopathos – and this is why Heidegger's task in that lecture course is to awaken that ground-attunement in his audience.

By the 1930s, Heidegger's Nazi-influenced nationalism and his turn to Hölderlin see him describing the ground-attunement of the German people at the time as 'holy mourning' or 'holy mourning in readied distress' ('*die heilig trauernde, bereite Bedrängnis*') (GA39: *passim*). Holy mourning mourns the flight of the gods after the Nietzschean death of God (GA39: 95). It is an internally complex ground-attunement that develops from abandonment (by the gods) to distress (at their absence) to readiness (for a new ground-attunement and a new arrival of the gods) (GA39: 103) (and it even contains its own counter-attunement (*Gegenstimmung*): joy (GA39: 148)). This ground-attunement is 'awakened in [Hölderlin's] late and most mature poetizing' (GA39: 146) (see Section 2.5).

Such communal, historical, and epochal ground-attunements are *at* the ground in a special way: they tune us into our ground in a way that determines not merely our philosophising but, more broadly, the community's entire understanding of being. Discussing holy mourning, Heidegger lays out four aspects of the essence of ground-attunements (GA39: 223): they (1) take us to the limits of entities and turn us either toward or away from the gods (compare turning toward or away from our being thrown); (2) bring us into relation to the Earth and the homeland; (3) open up entities as a whole, which is to say a world of possible meanings and matterings; and in doing so they (4) 'deliver[] our Dasein over to beyng, so that it must take up beyng, configure it and sustain it'. The core idea is that ground-attunements determine and attune – and in some sense *are* – worlds or understandings of being. So, when a poet brings about a new ground-attunement, they bring about a new world (see Section 2.5): 'The opening up of world occurs in ground-attunement. The power of a ground-attunement ... [is] *grounding*' (GA39: 141).

Even the most powerful grounding, however, eventually runs out of steam. The worlds opened up by ground-attunements lose their vitality, and since (as with ordinary attunements) there is only ever change of attunement, the place of the old ground-attunements will have to be taken by new ground-attunements. ('[O]nly a ground-attunement is capable of bringing about a change of attunement [*Umstimmung*] from the ground up – that is, a transformation of Dasein that amounts to a complete recreating of its exposure to entities, and thereby a recoining of beyng' (GA39: 142).) Since we are witnessing the decline of the original ontopathos experienced by the ancient Greeks and so transitioning out of the ambit of 'the first inception' or beginning, we are now awaiting the attuning of 'the other beginning' – a new age in our relationship to being (see Polt, 2006: 105–6). In a sort of perverted repetition of the original wonder, the ground-attunement in which we approach this other beginning is shock (*Erschrecken*): 'Shock lets us be taken aback by the very fact that entities *are*' (GA62: 20; GA45: 2). We are presumably shocked rather than astonished because in the fact that entities are we experience not the gift of being (as did the Greeks) but that being has abandoned us: 'being has abandoned and withdrawn itself from all "entities" and from whatever appeared as an entity' (GA65: 15). Being shows itself in its self-concealing (GA65: 15), to which we are attuned in restraint (*Verhaltenheit*) (GA45: 2). Indeed, being's self-concealing abandonment of us *gets to us* on multiple levels, lending this single ground-attunement many names and dimensions: not only shock and restraint but also diffidence (*Scheu*), presentiment (*Ahnung*), and foreboding (*Er-ahnen*) (GA65: 22 *et passim*). Thus: 'In the first beginning: wonder. In the other beginning: foreboding' (GA65: 20).

I have suggested that to be a ground-attunement is to be a way of being moved *by* the ground (of Dasein, of entities) and *at* the ground (of Dasein, of entities). Since the ground is (Dasein's) being, to be a ground-attunement is to be an ontopathos (rather than a way of being moved by entities, as are regular attunements). Being moved by one's being is also an autopathos or auto-affection (as is any ontopathos, in fact, insofar as being and Dasein are always correlated). As ontopathē and autopathē, ground-attunements are grounds in one final sense: they ground our becoming authentic.

3.5 Being Authentically Attuned

Being authentic (*eigentlich*) is one way to be a case of Dasein, in addition to being inauthentic (*uneigentlich*) (and, perhaps, being undifferentiated between the two (SZ: 43)). In our ordinary, everyday going about, we are absorbed in our engagement with entities and take the lead in how to make sense of things from *what one does* (i.e., from *das Man*). The latter is falling qua being inauthentic and the former is falling qua being-absorbed. As Heidegger tells the story in *Being and Time*, the ground-attunement of angst disrupts both types of falling. It brings us up out of the ontic so as to be affected by the ontological, giving us the insight into our being that is methodologically relevant for the existential analytic at the close of Division I. And it brings us up out of *das Man* so as to confront and take over our finitude in guilt and death, which *das Man* suppresses and which makes for the authentic self-disclosing that Heidegger explores in the first half of Division II. Like all disclosing, authentic self-disclosing involves understanding, talking, and finding – in this case, anticipating death, hearing the call of conscience, and either angst (SZ: 265–6, 296) or readiness for angst (SZ: 296, 297, 301, 385). Further, angst attunes the caller of conscience (SZ: 276ff.) and in some sense *is* being-towards-death (SZ: 266). Angst is thus the attunement of authenticity and experiencing it brings a case of Dasein to its authentic self-disclosing. The same sort of account is given in *The Fundamental Concepts of Metaphysics* when Heidegger analyses the ground-attunement of boredom: being exposed to our own temporal being in the ontopathos and autopathos of profound boredom amounts to being called to authentically take over our being as Dasein (GA29/30: 215). Ground-attunements such as boredom and angst ground authenticity by (i) disrupting falling and (ii) opening us to our being.

It is tempting to conclude that the distinction between ground-attunements and ordinary attunements maps onto the distinction between authentic attunement and inauthentic attunement. Thus, angst is authentic while fear is inauthentic (SZ: 189, 341).[19] What makes fear inauthentic is that, in this ordinary attunement, we are moved by entities. What makes angst authentic is that, in this ground-attunement, we are moved by our being. Thus we line up authenticity, ground-attunements, and the ontological on one side and contrast them to inauthenticity, ordinary attunements, and the ontic on the other (e.g., Vallega-Neu, 2019: 206).

But this account is too simplistic, for a number of reasons. First, it is not clear that sorting particular attunements into categories labelled 'authentic' or 'inauthentic' is the correct approach to authentic affectivity, given that authenticity and inauthenticity are supposed to be existentiell modifications of our everyday being-in-the-world (SZ: 130, 267) and so ways of bearing our attunements (rather than a matter of experiencing some attunements and not others). Second, the story as told relies on the fact that Heidegger runs together falling qua being-absorbed in entities and falling qua being inauthentically lost in *das Man*. It is this conflation that allows that story to slide from saying that ground-attunements disrupt falling absorption to saying that they disrupt inauthenticity and to saying that any entity-directed attunement is inauthentic. But not only are these moves unwarranted; their end point should strike us as implausible: being entity-directed and being inauthentic should not be equivalent. We are always factical, existing, being-amidst-entities – including, presumably, when we are authentic. So, third, there must be authentic ways of being-amidst-entities, including authentic ways of being moved by them. (At issue in this intuition is whether being authentic is not instead an exceptional condition of insight, an unsustainable 'moment of vision' (*Augenblick*) (SZ: 338) which disrupts our lives but does not carry over into them.)

Fourth, two of the ground-attunements that Heidegger discusses seem to be both directed toward the ontological *and* inauthentic. Our contemporary boredom, for example, is a ground-attunement in which our lack of ontological affliction gets to us (GA29/30: 244). Such boredom is a way of being attuned to our being, but it is attuned to a deficit or absence that should amount to an inauthenticity. So too for holy mourning and shock. In these ground-attunements, we are authentically moved by our true situation vis-à-vis-being.

---

[19] Heidegger also identifies, for example, respect (GA3: 159), equanimity (SZ: 345), and joy (SZ: 310) as authentic attunements and indifference as an inauthentic attunement (SZ: 345).

But our true situation vis-à-vis-being appears to be an inauthentic one, in which we are abandoned by the gods (GA39: 103) or being (GA65: 15). These are both counterexamples to the alignment of the ontological, and so ground-attunements, with the authentic. A more nuanced account of being authentically attuned is needed.

Such an account will explain what it is for things to get to us authentically, whether what gets to us is an entity or (our) being. The existing literature offers two approaches. On the first, we establish what Heidegger means by 'authenticity' and then work out how to apply this to our affective lives. On the second, we start with our affective lives, ask what it is for these to go well, and then work out how to coordinate this with Heidegger's account of authenticity. This second approach can be found in my Aristotelian account of authentic affectivity (Withy, 2015b), in which I draw on Heidegger's appropriation of Aristotle's account of the *pathē* and of excellence (*arētē*) in order to understand what it would be to experience excellent *pathē* or 'owned emotions'. The first approach can be found, for example, in Denis McManus's (2019) exploration of what it means to own our affective lives.

McManus argues that authentic affectivity is not a matter of choosing affects or of being affected consistently, but of being able to negotiate the variability and complexity of all the things that matter to us. He explains that it

> requires that I be open to my situation and its concretion in allowing my many emotions a voice in my deliberations, acknowledging rather than evading the full range of ways in which I am already attuned – tuned – to my situation, the many ways my situation already matters to me, touches me, and moves me, whether I wish to acknowledge that or not. (McManus, 2019: 144–5)

Being open to all my attunements and so to the various ways in which things matter to me, given my various pursuits, allows me to honestly navigate the various normative demands that fall on me and determine how to act in light of them. It allows me to make an 'all things considered judgement' about what to do, and making this judgement is my being authentic (McManus, 2019: 139). The inauthentic person, in contrast, denies or ignores the complexity of the normative demands they are subject to and follows *das Man* by feeling only 'as one does' in the situation (McManus, 2019: 143–4).

I agree that being authentically attuned requires resisting public norms about how one ought to be affected, but I do not think that McManus hits upon a genuinely authentic being affected. If authentic affectivity consists in 'allowing my many emotions a voice in my deliberations' (McManus, 2019: 144), then what is authentic or not is my deliberation and its handling of my emotions, not my emotions themselves. This may be an authentic affectivity but it is not being authentically affected. To be authentically affected is for my affects themselves to occur in such a way that they are authentic.

This is why I return to Aristotle (Withy, 2015b), who promises an account of what it is to experience *pathē* well or poorly, excellently or not, while acknowledging the fact that the *pathē* that we experience are not up to us (*Eth. Nic.* II.5). What opens the *pathē* to evaluation is their complex intentional structure: each has a how, when, whither, and about which (*das Wie, Wann, Wozu, und Worüber*) (GA18: 171; *Eth. Nic.* 1106b21–3)). So the *pathē* are not merely felt affects but ways of being open to various dimensions of our situation. They are evaluable in terms of how well they allow each dimension of the situation to show itself as it is. A *pathos* that achieves this excellently 'hits the mean' (*Eth. Nic.* 1107a1). Similarly, Heidegger's attunements are ways in which we discover things as mattering, and also disclose ourselves and the world, and they are evaluable as authentic or inauthentic in terms of whether they allow things to show themselves as they are, in themselves, and from themselves (cf. SZ: 28). At the very least, this means that they must discover and disclose without any distortion or manipulation – especially by the influence of *das Man*. (We can also be swept along inauthentically by the orator – the poet, the philosopher, or (especially ominously) the statesperson – manipulating a crowd.) Being authentically attuned requires, on the one hand, actively resisting these influences. On the other hand, it requires relaxing into the situation and allowing it to show up as it is and to move one as it does. To be authentically attuned is to *let* things get to us.

The challenge for this sort of account is reconciling it with what Heidegger says about authenticity, especially in *Being and Time*. The difficulty for accounts such as McManus's is plausibly tying the stance on authenticity to what it is to be affected and attuned. (Since each approach comes from a different direction – authenticity for the one, affectivity for the other – it is possible that they will ultimately be reconciled.) And if both accounts avoid the first three problems that I pointed out earlier, they do not address the fourth: what to say about ground-attunements such as boredom, holy mourning, and shock, which appear to authentically open us to a shared way of being that is inauthentic. It also remains to reconcile these approaches to authentic attunement with the fact that ground-attunements bring us to authenticity. What is it about being exposed to our being, in angst or in boredom, that allows us to incorporate all our emotions into our deliberation or to let each aspect of the situation show itself as it is in itself? Or was the very idea of authentic attunements that are not ground-attunements a mistake? These questions all open up onto broader interpretive questions about Heidegger's views. Many questions remain; much work is yet to be done.

4 Uptake

Heidegger's account of being affected by things has received some limited but promising uptake in philosophy, psychology, and associated areas. Various parts of it have begun to contribute to conversations, been confirmed by empirical research, and come in for criticism. How we assess those criticisms and contributions depends on what we think the account is about and what it is trying to do. I have stressed throughout this Element that Heidegger is not primarily interested in theorising about emotions and moods; he is not aiming to contribute to either the philosophy or the psychology of emotion. He is trying to understand how things – including and especially ontological phenomena – can get to us. From this perspective, some of the criticisms that are frequently levelled against Heidegger's account miss the mark (Section 4.1). They hold his account to standards that it was not designed to meet. By the same token, Heidegger's departure from familiar approaches to emotions and moods makes his account a potential source of promising insight (Section 4.2).

4.1 Criticisms

The most damning criticism of Heidegger's account of *Befindlichkeit* in *Being and Time* comes from Dahlstrom, who describes affectivity as 'missing in action' – 'in some cases conspicuously, perhaps even egregiously' – in that text (Dahlstrom, 2019: 111). His evidence is that there is little in *Being and Time* about recognisable feelings or emotions. We do not see discussions of the emotional dimensions of understanding or being-with-others, or of the felt dimensions of being subject to *das Man*, falling, authenticity, and angst (Dahlstrom, 2019: 112–18). Although some of these are 'highly emotional experiences' (Dahlstrom, 2019: 114), there is 'no elaboration of how it feels to have those experiences' (Dahlstrom, 2019: 114). But Dahlstrom is looking for the wrong thing if he is looking for the felt dimension of experience. As we have seen, what Heidegger is seeking when he considers our capacity to be affected by things is much broader and more fundamental. Still, the account of *Befindlichkeit* as allowing things to get to us had to be wrested from the text and reconstructed, so it is hard to disagree with Dahlstrom's overall assessment that *Befindlichkeit* is undertheorised in *Being and Time* (and hardly theorised at all elsewhere). The most that can be said in response is that it is not the only thing that is undertheorised there.

Most notoriously undertheorised in *Being and Time*, and in Heidegger's thought generally, is the body. Heidegger has come in for particular criticism for leaving the body out of his account of affectivity (e.g., Freeman, 2016: 253; Ratcliffe, 2013: 171, 2008: 55). Ratcliffe (2013: 171) explains: 'This is a serious omission when it comes to understanding mood, as some account is surely needed of what moods actually *are*, in addition to what they do, and of how they relate to the feeling body.' So strongly worded, however, the criticism misses the mark – as does the response that, because of the manifestly central role of the body in affectivity, the body is actually everywhere, implicitly, in Heidegger's account (Stolorow, 2014; Vallega-Neu, 2019: 207). I have argued that the phenomenon that Heidegger is interested in is that of being moved. We can be moved in ways that do not essentially or centrally involve the body – for example, when an impending deadline prompts me to turn my attention to a problem. There is likely some felt dimension to this – a certain urgency, perhaps – but it is not obvious that that is what my being moved *consists* in (cf. Withy, 2019: 171). (Or, recall Shockey's (2016: 19) argument that angst as an ontopathos and autopathos involves no felt dimension.)

That said, at least a significant portion of our experience of being moved by things *does* involve bodily feeling. Some account of this is needed. Aristotle, of course, holds that 'there seems to be no case in which the soul can act or be acted upon without involving the body; e.g., anger, courage, appetite, and sensation generally' (*De Anima* 403a5–7) (with *thinking* being the not insignificant exception). Heidegger acknowledges this, at least for the genesis of the *pathē* (GA18: 203). He allows that angst 'is often conditioned by "physiological" factors' (SZ: 190; cf. GA20: 401) but later notes that attunement (*Gestimmtheit*) cannot be produced physiologically but only 'triggered' (*ausgelöst*) (GA89: 244). Heidegger discusses his neglect of the body in the *Zollikon Seminars* (1959–69) but never makes good on the omission.

Heidegger also fails to offer what we expect when it comes to the range of affective phenomena that he considers (Aho, 2019: 13) – and those that he does consider can appear to be insufficiently treated. Lauren Freeman (2016: 253), for example, worries that 'his account of mood is *too limited* in that it considers only a few moods at length, namely fear . . ., anxiety, and boredom'. Ratcliffe (2008: 52) shares this worry and adds that 'some of the predicaments that Heidegger does discuss require more fine-grained differentiation', such as angst, which arguably 'encompasses a range of subtly different experiences' (cf. Ratcliffe, 2013: 171–2) – and, Elpidorou and Freeman (2019: 178) add, Heidegger's profound boredom 'cannot be seamlessly assimilated to any known category of boredom'. But why would Heidegger want to assimilate to known categories or match the differentiation of phenomena provided in psychology? Notice that when Ratcliffe (2013: 171–2) attempts to answer this question, he changes the subject:

> Given the central methodological role that anxiety plays in *Being and Time*, it would be problematic if Heidegger's description of it failed to discriminate between several different forms of anxiety. Of course, one might retort that there is a difference between clinical anxiety and the kind of deep anxiety addressed by Heidegger. Real anxiety, as Heidegger says, is rare. However, it is important not to trivialise the kinds of anxiety that are reported in psychiatric contexts.

The passage begins with the methodological role of angst in *Being and Time* and ends with a clinical imperative. It does not explain why the type of phenomenological differentiation that is important in psychiatric contexts is relevant for Heidegger's methodology. That methodology and its goals provide the appropriate standards against which to assess the range of phenomena that Heidegger discusses and the detail in which he does so. Naturally, Heidegger's account might be inadequate by the lights of those standards. (Although Heidegger seems not to think so, at least in *Being and Time*: 'The different modes of *Befindlichkeit* and the ways in which they are interconnected in their foundations cannot be interpreted within the problematic of the present investigation' (SZ: 128).) My point is that the clinical, diagnostic, and theoretical needs of psychology are – like the phenomenological needs of the philosophy of emotion – the wrong standards to which to hold his account.

I suspect that Heidegger's discussions of attunements are frequently held to the wrong standards because he labels his philosophical project 'phenomenology'. Heard in a contemporary sense, a phenomenology of being affected would offer a descriptive philosophy of emotion – one that describes what it feels like to experience a wide range of emotions, or any emotion at all, and one that is beholden to the psychological and folk-psychological phenomena. But Heidegger is not engaged in phenomenology in this sense. The reasons that Heidegger calls his project 'phenomenology', and in what sense this project is a continuation of Edmund Husserl's phenomenological project, are much disputed. But it is clear that Heidegger is not doing phenomenology in any straightforwardly descriptive sense. (If he were, his critics would be correct that he does an astonishingly poor job of it.)

The same response applies to criticisms that take Heidegger to task for not tracking our folk-psychological distinctions between emotions (as intentionally-directed episodic states) and moods (as diffuse, longer-lasting, nonintentional states). Freeman, for example, responds to this charge on Heidegger's behalf by absolving him of having to meet the usual standards of clarity and precision on so-called phenomenological grounds. She forgives Heidegger his 'sloppiness' and writes (Freeman, 2016: 254) that 'I do not believe that philosophical tidiness (or, conceptual precision) is the most important virtue toward which we should strive, especially if our goal is to provide an account of emotion and mood that actually maps onto the phenomena as we experience them' in all their 'messiness'. But Heidegger neither succeeds in this descriptive phenomenological project nor fails to track the folk-psychological categories. Neither captures the project that he is attempting to undertake – which, as Daniela Vallega-Neu (2019: 205–6) points out in this context, aims at fundamental ontology. So, neither provides the appropriate standard against which Heidegger's project can be said to either fail or succeed.

Heidegger does not consider folk psychology to be a good guide to understanding what it is to be us because it involves both fallen and inauthentic self-misunderstanding. He is also consistently critical of the psychology and philosophy of emotion of his day. He sees the field as inheriting the Aristotelian lineage of insights about the *pathē*, which runs through the Stoics, Augustine, and into the Middle Ages and then, via the Renaissance, into modernity (GA20: 393; SZ: 139; GA18: 177–8; cf. Ruin, 2000). (Only Wilhelm Dilthey, according to Heidegger, made any real post-Aristotelian philosophical progress in treating the affects and 'characteriz[ing] their significance for psychological states' (GA18: 178). But Heidegger does not, as far as I can see, explore Dilthey's ideas.) Heidegger thinks that Aristotle's insights have not always been properly or fully understood and that 'affects and feelings [have] come under the theme of psychical phenomena, functioning as a third class of these, usually along with ideation and volition. They sink to the level of accompanying phenomena' (SZ: 139). This sort of view misses the significance of the affects as that in which things matter to and move us, which places them prior to and fundamental for volition and cognition (see Section 4.2). It does so because it misses the entire context of being-in-the-world, which is occluded when we take ourselves to be psyches:

> What are otherwise called 'feelings' and 'emotions' and treated as a special class of lived experiences remain unclarified in their primary structure of being as long as one does not take up the task of exposing the basic constitution of Dasein and here in particular its disclosedness, so as to draw these phenomena back into this constitutive structure. . . . Even the most extensive psychology will never unravel the authentic structure of these phenomena, because psychology in principle does not enter into the dimension of the structure of Dasein as such. (GA20: 353)

If you miss the ways in which we open up and dwell in meaning and mattering, you miss the phenomenon of being affected. This makes traditional approaches to the affects in both philosophy and psychology flawed from the start.

The task of a project such as Heidegger's that *does* begin from our being-in-the-world is to work out what follows from that. As Heidegger explains, '[i]t is not a matter of taking up an opposite stance to psychology and delimiting more correctly a kind of emotional experience, thus improving psychology, but rather a matter of first opening up a general perspective upon the *Dasein* of the human being' (GA29/30: 101). Nonetheless, what becomes manifest in this general perspective can be taken up and made use of by those pursuing different projects, including in psychology and the philosophy of emotions – and beyond.

4.2 Contributions

Heidegger's account of being affected has contributed to, and can continue to contribute to, various parts of philosophy, psychology, and other disciplines. It does not make its contribution, however, by sharing in those pursuits – by taking up their projects, assumptions, and vocabularies and inhabiting their world of meanings and matterings. Heidegger's account retains its own goals and vocabulary, its own set of meanings and matterings. On the one hand, this makes communicating its ideas difficult and calls for some translation. On the other hand, the very idiosyncrasy of the approach lends it value. Heidegger's account is indifferent to canonical debates and cuts against the grain of the usual questions, cutting up and cutting through sedimented patterns of thought and inquiry. In this final section, I highlight some of the ways in which these cuts have made an impact.

The biggest impacts made by Heidegger's account of affectivity are probably in the psychological disciplines and the parts of philosophy that abut them. I begin with these because they were also the earliest impacts. (I will return to more contemporary impacts at the end of the section). Two Swiss psychiatrists – Ludwig Binswanger (1881–1966) and Medard Boss (1903–90)– were, separately, early adopters of Heidegger's account of us as Dasein and each worked to adapt it to serve as a fresh foundation for psychology and its therapeutic practices.[20] Dispensing with traditional psychology's Cartesian and naturalistic assumptions, both aimed to understand patients and their struggles in terms of their being-in-the-world. In an effusive letter, Boss wrote to Heidegger that '[i]n the basic structures of the way of human existing which you elaborated, I recognized the most reliable outline of an art of healing' (GA89: 365). But while Boss, Binswanger, and others were inspired by the account of being-in-the-world in general, including its account of affectivity, neither engaged with the specifics of that account directly and in detail.

One of the Cartesian assumptions to be destabilised is that we are primarily *thinking* entities. Heidegger's focus on being affected underscores that, before we are thinking, we are affected by things. This insight drives Dreyfus's appeal to

---

[20] Boss corresponded extensively with Heidegger and regularly hosted the latter at his home in Zollikon, Switzerland between 1959 and 1969, where Heidegger offered seminars to psychiatrists and psychotherapists. Notes from those seminars and associated discussions were later published as GA89.

Heidegger in his critique of early attempts at artificial intelligence in the United States in the 1960s and 1970s. The general claim is that computers built to think about objects cannot and do not disclose or otherwise access a world. Worlds are opened up and structured by taking up pursuits that we care about, and only on the basis of world can we discover entities or know objects. Dreyfus (1992: 261) writes that '[t]he human world … is prestructured in terms of human purposes and concerns in such a way that what counts as an object or is significant about an object already is a function of, or embodies, that concern. This cannot be matched by a computer, which can deal only with universally defined, i.e., context-free, objects.' Entities cannot be known if they do not matter.

Haugeland (1998: 47) famously put this point, and the critique of artificial intelligence that it implies, by saying '[t]he trouble with artificial intelligence is that computers don't give a damn'. (Blattner (2006: 37) correctly insists that 'Heidegger would want to modify [the formulation] thus: the problem with artificial intelligence is that computers neither do nor don't give a damn.') Giving a damn includes, first, caring about the world and being motivated to understand things at all. It includes, second, caring about getting things right – being disturbed when one might not have; refusing to accept apparent errors, impossibilities, and contradictions; feeling obligated and moved to correct, dissolve, and resolve those errors, impossibilities, and contradictions; being delighted when one has (provisionally) done so, and so on. Haugeland argues that this flavour of giving a damn – taking responsibility for getting things right – is necessary for genuine intentionality and he holds that thinking machines cannot do it. He writes that 'cognitive science – and especially cognitive science inspired by the idea of computation – has been effectively oblivious to this essential connection between cognition and responsibility' (Haugeland, 2013: 268). With this, it has been oblivious to the importance to cognition of being affected.

It is not just that a knower must be moved to know, and be moved to know well. A knower must be moved *in order to* know. Heidegger holds that attunements are the 'presupposition for', and 'medium' of, thinking and acting (GA29/30: 101) and thus come *'prior to* all cognition and volition' (SZ: 136) as their condition of possibility. Ratcliffe finds confirmation of this claim in contemporary neuropsychology. He reports on experiments showing that 'emotions constitute a kind of cradle within which cognition rests' (Ratcliffe, 2002: 296), 'constraining and structuring' (Ratcliffe, 2002: 297) what is available for thought by showing some things to be relevant to it and others not to be relevant to it. This shows that 'emotions don't just cloud reason (although they can do); they are also a prerequisite for successful reasoning, in that they tune us to the world, making it relevant to us by opening up certain possibilities for explicit deliberation and closing off others' (Ratcliffe, 2002: 297–8). As Heidegger puts it: 'Any cognitive determining has its existential–ontological constitution in the *Befindlichkeit* of being-in-the-world, but pointing this out is not to be confused with attempting to surrender science ontically to "feeling"' (SZ: 138). Instead, it offers science 'an informative perspectival reorientation' (Ratcliffe, 2002: 295).

(As Ratcliffe explains, it follows from this view that '[a]ny neurological damage to the working emotions therefore has a profound effect on human reasoning, which essentially takes place relative to a background of moods and emotions' (Ratcliffe, 2002: 296). This might be why we see cases, such as that of Phineas Gage, in which 'emotional impairment is reliably coupled with a catastrophic failure of practical reasoning' (Ratcliffe, 2002: 296). Ratcliffe goes on to consider Capgras' Syndrome, which he takes to disrupt one's foundational affective being-in-the-world and as a result to impair one's ability to identify and categorise objects (Ratcliffe, 2002: 300ff.).)

If being moved by things that matter is a prerequisite for discovering them or thinking about them, then attunements must come earlier and be situated more centrally in the story of knowing or making sense of things than we might have thought. Traditionally, affects are positioned as subsequent to cognition of objects, as an unnecessary, subjective, and distorting layer or lens that clouds or colours a pure, objective, foundational access to entities as they are. Such objectivity turns out to be a fantasy, as we learned over the course of twentieth-century thought. Heidegger helped to cut the ties to that fantasy by insisting that the subjectivity of affectivity is also a mirage. As he conceives it, being affected cuts across the distinction between subjective and objective and so obliterates it. Heidegger writes of attunement that it 'comes neither from "outside" nor from "inside", but arises out of being-in-the-world' (SZ: 136; cf. GA29/30: 100). Similarly, Gibson's affordances are 'neither an objective property nor a subjective property' but are 'both if you like' (Gibson, 1986: 129). He goes on: 'An affordance cuts across the dichotomy of subjective–objective and helps us to understand its inadequacy. It is equally a fact of the environment and a fact of behavior. It is both physical and psychical, yet neither. An affordance points both ways, to the environment and to the observer' (Gibson, 1986: 129). This is why affordances are perceived directly and immediately and are not to be conceived as layers subjectively placed on objective features of the environment (Gibson, 1986: 127, 140). So too for solicitations or matterings, which are perceived directly and immediately in attunements. They are what we encounter first: the threat of rain comes before any measurable precipitation. (The humanoid android, of course, has it the other way around.) It is in this sense that 'we must as a general principle leave the primary discovery of the world to "bare attunement"' (SZ: 138).

Like Aristotle's *pathē*, Heidegger's attunements take place where we and entities meet. This view encourages us to move the traditional affects out of the head and into the world, and it is this move that has perhaps had the most impact on the philosophy of emotion and related areas of philosophy and psychology (Freeman, 2014). To take a telling example: Slaby notes that Heidegger's account 'provides ample [re]enforcement for the situated affectivity movement that has gained much currency in recent years' (Slaby, 2017: 22). Situated views of affectivity in philosophy hold that affects are not wholly internal matters of our individual minds or brains but have to do also with our bodies and social relationships. Such views are readily criticisable for not noticing that these insights are already available in the Aristotelian tradition (Stephan and Walter, 2020), and Slaby (2017: 22) rightly points out that Heidegger's view is 'more radical with regard to situatedness than most proposals in this trend' (noting especially the temporal situatedness of our affective lives).

But the primary respect in which our being affected is situated on Heidegger's account is in our world-opening. We are not just knowers and feelers, equipped with bodies and social relationships, who are intentionally directed toward entities. We are that because we disclose worlds.[21] To be attuned is to dwell in a context of possible ways in which things can matter to us. It is this world-disclosing and world-dwelling aspect of our affective lives that has been taken up in phenomenological studies of psychiatry, illness, and psychopathology, in order to understand the altered worlds of mattering found in illness (Svenaeus, 2000), chronic pain (Kush & Ratcliffe, 2018: 76), anxiety (Ratcliffe, 2015; Aho, 2019: ch. 6), depression (Ratcliffe, 2015; Aho, 2019: ch. 2), depersonalisation/derealisation (Ratcliffe, 2008: ch. 6), and others.[22]

In particular, those phenomena that are understood as affective disorders, disruptions, or breakdowns are frequently conceptualised as involving a transformed world due to the fact that soliciting breaks down or the field of possible solicitations is altered in some way – often in the way found in the ground-attunements of angst and boredom (Sections 3.2, 3.3, and 3.4). Vocational soliciting might break down, leaving one unable to take up any pursuit (e.g., Aho, 2019: 33) and so open up a world. Or, the field of solicitings opened up might be altered, such that certain possibilities of soliciting are transformed, suspended, or eradicated. Thus, Ratcliffe explains that people experiencing severe depression 'often report that all sense of practical significance has vanished, and alongside it, a sense of the potential for emotional connectedness with other people. At the same time, other ways of

---

[21] The one dimension of Heidegger's account of finding and attunement that has not, to my knowledge, received any uptake is the idea that attunements are self-disclosing. Interestingly, the passages in which Heidegger insists that cognition is subsequent to attunement are passages in which he speaks of us as finding ourselves attuned (and not: discovering entities) (SZ: 134–6; cf. GA18: 262). This suggests that the focus on intentionality and discovering entities, at least as far as Heidegger is concerned, is misplaced.

[22] The authors cited draw directly and explicitly on Heidegger's account of being affected. Many others are indirectly influenced by that account, including through the authors mentioned.

mattering can become more pronounced, even all encompassing [*sic*]. For instance, everything might be encountered through a sense of threat' (Ratcliffe, 2013: 160). Most recognisably, in depression, 'happiness is no longer part of one's emotional repertoire' (Ratcliffe, 2010: 609), having been eradicated from the field of possible solicitings and so from the world.

Anthony Vincent Fernandez has argued against Ratcliffe that certain types of experience involve not only breakdowns of solicitations or distinctive modes of attunement but alterations in the very structure of *Befindlichkeit* itself (Fernandez, 2014). He gives the example of people diagnosed with major depressive disorder and suggests that 'rather than understanding their depression as a kind of mood or feeling' and so as a mode of *Befindlichkeit*, 'it is more accurately understood as an erosion of the degree to which they are situated in and through moods' (Fernandez, 2014: 597) and so as a 'degradation of the existential structure' of *Befindlichkeit* (Fernandez, 2014: 605). Such depression is, he suggests, not a way of being situated but a becoming 'de-situated' (Fernandez, 2018: 39). The claim is that it is possible for someone to no longer be finding – to no longer be determined by the existential structure of *Befindlichkeit* (Fernandez, 2018: 39).

The argument is unpersuasive. (It does not distinguish breakdowns of a structure that amount to suspending all its modal manifestations from breakdowns of that structure itself. In other words: Fernandez (2014: 606) runs together 'the absence of moods and situatedness', of *Stimmungen* and of *Befindlichkeit*, when he should distinguish the two absences.) But it is nonetheless an idea worth considering. What would it be – if anything – to no longer be finding? William James (1983: 927) quotes Wilhelm Griesinger paraphrasing 'melancholic patients': "'I see, I hear!" such patients say, "but the objects do not reach me"'.[23] Kevin Aho (2019: 28) quotes a person suffering from depression who writes of seeing vibrant autumnal leaves: 'nothing in me was touched'.[24] Can we take these descriptions at face value? What would it be not to be touched by *any* things? And who would we be if, further, we *could not* be reached or moved – if entities could not get to us at all?

That we can barely countenance an answer to this last question shows how foundational our being affected is to our being-in-the-world. That we can raise the question shows what new possibilities for thinking Heidegger's account of being affected both affords and solicits. (For more, see Slaby, 2021: 249). These new possibilities have transformed the world of our thinking about being affected and allowed us to tune in to and be moved by this most fundamental feature of our being – to be moved, that is, by the very fact that things get to us.

---

[23] James gives this reference: Griesinger, W. 1845. *Die Pathologie und Therapie der psychischen Krankheiten*, §50, 98. The passage is also quoted by Aho (2019: 28–9) and others.

[24] Aho gives this reference: Karp, D. 1996. *Speaking of Sadness: Depression, Disconnection, and the Meaning of Illness*. Oxford: Oxford University Press, 61.

References

Primary Texts

SZ   *Sein und Zeit*. Tübingen: Niemeyer, 1967. English translation: *Being and Time*. Translated by J. Macquarrie & E. Robinson. New York: Harper Collins, 1962.

GA3   *Kant und das Problem der Metaphysik. Gesamtausgabe*, Volume 3. Edited by F.-W. von Herrmann. Frankfurt: Klostermann, 1991. English translation: *Kant and the Problem of Metaphysics*, fifth edition. Translated by R. Taft. Bloomington: Indiana University Press, 1997.

GA4   *Erläuterungen zu Hölderlins Dichtung. Gesamtausgabe*, Volume 4. Edited by F.-W. von Herrmann. Frankfurt: Klostermann, 1981, 1996. English translation: *Elucidations of Hölderlin's Poetry*. Translated by K. Hoeller. Amherst, NY: Humanity Books, 2000.

GA9   *Wegmarken. Gesamtausgabe*, Volume 9. Edited by F.-W. von Herrmann. Frankfurt: Klostermann, 1976. English translation: *Pathmarks*. Edited by W. McNeill. Cambridge: Cambridge University Press, 1998.

GA11   *Identität und Differenz. Gesamtausgabe*, Volume 11. Edited by F.-W. von Herrmann. Frankfurt: Klostermann, 2006. Partial English translation (GA11: 3–26, 'Was ist das – die Philosophie?' (1955)): *What Is Philosophy?* Translated by W. Kluback & J. T. Wilde. New Haven, CT: College and University Press, 1956.

GA18   *Grundbegriffe der aristotelischen Philosophie. Gesamtausgabe*, Volume 18. Edited by M. Michalski. Frankfurt: Klostermann, 2002. English translation: *Basic Concepts of Aristotelian Philosophy*. Translated by R. D. Metcalf & M. B. Tanzer. Bloomington: Indiana University Press, 2009.

GA20   *Prolegomena zur Geschichte des Zeitbegriffs. Gesamtausgabe*, Volume 20. Edited by P. Jaeger. Frankfurt: Klostermann, 1979. English translation: *History of the Concept of Time: Prolegomena*. Translated by T. Kisiel. Bloomington: Indiana University Press, 1985.

GA29/30   *Die Grundbegriffe der Metaphysik: Welt, Endlichkeit, Einsamkeit. Gesamtausgabe*, Volume 29/30. Edited by F.-W. von Herrmann. Frankfurt: Klostermann, 1983. English translation: *The*

Fundamental Concepts of Metaphysics: World, Finitude, Solitude. Translated by W. McNeill & N. Walker. Bloomington: Indiana University Press, 1995.

GA39   *Hölderlins Hymnen 'Germanien' und 'Der Rhein'. Gesamtausgabe*, Volume 39. Edited by S. Ziegler. Frankfurt: Klostermann, 1980. English translation: *Hölderlin's Hymns 'Germania' and 'The Rhine'.* Translated by W. McNeill & J. Ireland. Bloomington: Indiana University Press, 2014.

GA40   *Einführung in die Metaphysik. Gesamtausgabe*, Volume 40. Edited by P. Jaeger. Frankfurt: Klostermann, 1983. English translation: *Introduction to Metaphysics.* Translated by G. Fried & R. Polt. New Haven, CT: Yale University Press, 2000; second edition 2014.

GA45   *Grundfragen der Philosophie: Ausgewählte 'Probleme' der 'Logik'. Gesamtausgabe*, Volume 45. Edited by F.-W. von Hermann, second edition. Frankfurt: Klostermann, 1992. English translation: *Basic Questions of Philosophy: Selected 'Problems' of 'Logic'.* Translated by R. Rojcewicz & A. Schuwer. Bloomington: Indiana University Press, 1994.

GA60   *Phänomenologie des religiösen Lebens. Gesamtausgabe*, Volume 60. Edited by M. Jung, T. Regehly, & C. Strube. Frankfurt: Klostermann, 1995. English translation: *The Phenomenology of Religious Life.* Translated by M. Fritsch and J. A. Gosetti-Ferencei. Bloomington: Indiana University Press, 2004.

GA65   *Beiträge zur Philosophie (vom Ereignis). Gesamtausgabe*, Volume 65. Edited by F.-W. von Hermann. Frankfurt: Klostermann, 1989. English translation: *Contributions to Philosophy (of the Event).* Translated by R. Rojcewicz & D. Vallega-Neu. Bloomington: Indiana University Press, 2012.

GA71   *Das Ereignis. Gesamtausgabe*, Volume 71. Edited by F.-W. von Hermann. Frankfurt: Klostermann, 2009. English translation: *The Event.* Translated by R. Rojcewicz. Bloomington: Indiana University Press, 2013.

GA89   *Zollikoner Seminare. Gesamtausgabe*, Volume 89. Edited by P. Trawny. Frankfurt: Klostermann, 2017. English translation: *Zollikon Seminars: Protocols – Conversations – Letters.* Edited by M. Boss. Translated by F. Mayr & R. Askay. Evanston, IL: Northwestern University Press, 2001.

Secondary Texts

Agosta, L. (2010). Heidegger's 1924 Clearing of the Affects Using Aristotle's *Rhetoric*, Book II. *Philosophy Today*, Winter, 333–45.

Aho, K., ed. (2018). *Existential Medicine: Essays on Health and Illness*. London: Rowman & Littlefield.

Aho, K. (2019). *Contexts of Suffering: A Heideggerian Approach to Psychopathology*. London: Rowman & Littlefield.

Aristotle. (1984a). *Nicomachean Ethics*. Translated by W. D. Ross. In *The Complete Works of Aristotle, Volume Two: The Revised Oxford Translation*, edited by J. Barnes. Princeton, NJ: Princeton University Press, pp. ii–170.

Aristotle, (1984b). *On the Soul*. Translated by J. A. Smith. In *The Complete Works of Aristotle, Volume One: The Revised Oxford Translation*, edited by J. Barnes. Princeton, NJ: Princeton University Press, pp. ii–64.

Aristotle. (1984c). *Politics*. Translated by B. Jowett. In *The Complete Works of Aristotle, Volume Two: The Revised Oxford Translation*, edited by J. Barnes. Princeton, NJ: Princeton University Press, pp. ii–175.

Aristotle. (1984d). *Rhetoric*. Translated by W. Rhys Roberts. In *The Complete Works of Aristotle, Volume Two: The Revised Oxford Translation*, edited by J. Barnes. Princeton, NJ: Princeton University Press, pp. ii–143.

Aristotle. (1996). *Metaphysics: Books I–IX*. Translated by H. Tredennick. Cambridge, MA: Harvard University Press.

Augustine. (2019). *Confessions*. Translated by T. Williams. Indianapolis, IN: Hackett.

Balaska, M. (in press). *Anxiety and Wonder: On Being Human*. London: Bloomsbury.

Beistegui, M. de (2000). Boredom: Between Existence and History: On Heidegger's Pivotal *The Fundamental Concepts of Metaphysics*. *Journal of the British Society for Phenomenology*, 31(2), 145–58.

Blattner, W. (1994). The Concept of Death in *Being and Time*. *Man and World*, 27(1), 49–70.

Blattner, W. (1999). *Heidegger's Temporal Idealism*. Cambridge: Cambridge University Press.

Blattner, W. (2006). *Heidegger's Being and Time*. London: Continuum.

Blattner, W. (2024). *Heidegger's Being and Time*, second edition. London: Continuum.

Carlisle, C. (2015). A Tale of Two Footnotes: Heidegger and the Question of Kierkegaard. In *Heidegger, Authenticity and the Self: Themes from Division Two of Being and Time*, edited by D. McManus. London: Routledge, pp. 37–55.

Carman, T. (2003). *Heidegger's Analytic: Interpretation, Discourse, and Authenticity in Being and Time*. Cambridge: Cambridge University Press.

Carnap, R. (1931). Überwindung der Metaphysik durch logische Analyse der Sprache. *Erkenntnis*, 2(1), 219–41.

Crowell, S. (2013). *Normativity and Phenomenology in Husserl and Heidegger*. Cambridge: Cambridge University Press.

Dahlstrom, D. O. (2001). *Heidegger's Concept of Truth*. Cambridge: Cambridge University Press.

Dahlstrom, D. O. (2002). Scheler's Critique of Heidegger's Fundamental Ontology. In *Max Scheler's Acting Persons: New Perspectives*, edited by S. Schneck. Amsterdam: Rodopi, pp. 67–92.

Dahlstrom, D. O. (2019). Missing in Action: Affectivity in *Being and Time*. In *Heidegger on Affect*, edited by C. Hadjioannou. Cham: Palgrave Macmillan, pp. 105–26.

Dreyfus, H. L. (1991). *Being-in-the-World: A Commentary on Heidegger's Being and Time, Division I*. Cambridge, MA: The MIT Press.

Dreyfus, H. L. (1992). *What Computers Still Can't Do: A Critique of Artificial Reason*. Cambridge, MA: The MIT Press.

Elpidorou, A. & Freeman, L. (2015). Affectivity in Heidegger I: Moods and Emotions in *Being and Time*. *Philosophy Compass*, 10(10), 661–71.

Elpidorou, A. & Freeman, L. (2019). Is Profound Boredom Boredom? In *Heidegger on Affect*, edited by C. Hadjioannou. Cham: Palgrave Macmillan, pp. 177–204.

Emad, P. (1985). Boredom as Limit and Disposition. *Heidegger Studies*, 1, 63–78.

Fernandez, A. V. (2014). Depression as Existential Feeling or De-Situatedness? Distinguishing Structure from Mode in Psychopathology. *Phenomenology and the Cognitive Sciences*, 13(4), 595–612.

Fernandez, A. V. (2018). Beyond the Ontological Difference: Heidegger, Binswanger, and the Future of Existential Analysis. In *Existential Medicine: Essays on Health and Illness*, edited by K. Aho. London: Rowman & Littlefield, pp. 27–42.

Freeman, L. (2014). Toward a Phenomenology of Mood. *Southern Journal of Philosophy*, 52(4), 445–76.

Freeman, L. (2016). Defending a Heideggerian Account of Mood. In *Philosophy of Mind and Phenomenology: Conceptual and Empirical Approaches*, edited by D. O. Dahlstrom, A. Elpidorou, & W. Hopp. New York: Routledge, pp. 247–67.

Freeman, L. & Elpidorou, A. (2015). Affectivity in Heidegger II: Temporality, Boredom, and Beyond. *Philosophy Compass*, 10(10), 672–84.

Gibson, J. (1986). The Theory of Affordances. In *The Ecological Approach to Visual Perception*. Hillsdale, NJ: Lawrence Erlbaum Associates, pp. 127–43.

Golob, S. (2017). Methodological Anxiety: Heidegger on Moods and Emotions. In *Thinking About Emotions: A Philosophical History*, edited by A. Cohen & R. Stern. Oxford: Oxford University Press, pp. 253–71.

Gouldman, G. (1966). Lyrics to 'Bus Stop', recorded and performed by The Hollies. Parlophone.

Guignon, C. (2003 (1984)). Moods in Heidegger's *Being and Time*. In *What Is an Emotion? Classic and Contemporary Readings*, second edition, edited by R. C. Solomon. Oxford: Oxford University Press, pp. 181–90.

Hadjioannou, C. (2013). *Befindlichkeit* as Retrieval of Aristotelian *Diathesis*: Heidegger Reading Aristotle in the Marburg Years. In *Heideggers Marburger Zeit: Themen, Argumente, Konstellationen*, edited by T. Keiling. Frankfurt: Vittorio Klostermann, pp. 223–35.

Hadjioannou, C. (2019a). Angst as Evidence: Shifting Phenomenology's Measure. In *Heidegger on Affect*, edited by C. Hadjioannou. Cham: Palgrave Macmillan, pp. 69–104.

Hadjioannou, C., ed. (2019b). *Heidegger on Affect*. Cham: Palgrave Macmillan.

Haugeland, J. (1989). Dasein's Disclosedness. *Southern Journal of Philosophy*, XXVIII (Supplement), 51–73.

Haugeland, J. (1998). *Having Thought: Essays in the Metaphysics of Mind*. Cambridge, MA: Harvard University Press.

Haugeland, J. (2000). Truth and Finitude: Heidegger's Transcendental Existentialism. In *Heidegger, Authenticity, and Modernity: Essays in Honor of Hubert L. Dreyfus, Volume 1*, edited by M. A. Wrathall & J. Malpas. Cambridge, MA: The MIT Press, pp. 43–78.

Haugeland, J. (2013). *Dasein Disclosed: John Haugeland's Heidegger*, edited by J. Rouse. Cambridge, MA: Harvard University Press.

James, W. (1983). *The Principles of Psychology*. Cambridge, MA: Harvard University Press.

Käufer, S. (2001). On Heidegger on Logic. *Continental Philosophy Review*, 34(4), 455–76.

Käufer, S. (2005). The Nothing and the Ontological Difference in Heidegger's *What Is Metaphysics? Inquiry*, 48(6), 482–506.

Keane, N. (2019). The Affects of Rhetoric and Reconceiving the Nature of Possibility. In *Heidegger on Affect*, edited by C. Hadjioannou. Cham: Palgrave Macmillan, pp. 47–67.

Kierkegaard, S. (1981 (1844)). *The Concept of Anxiety: A Simple Psychologically Orienting Deliberation on the Dogmatic Issue of Hereditary Sin*. Translated by R. Thomte & A. B. Anderson. Princeton, NJ: Princeton University Press.

Kisiel, T. (1993). *The Genesis of Heidegger's Being and Time*. Berkeley: University of California Press.

Kush, M. & Ratcliffe, M. (2018). The World of Chronic Pain: A Dialog. In *Existential Medicine: Essays on Health and Illness*, edited by K. Aho. London: Rowman & Littlefield, pp. 61–80.

Magid, O. (2016). The Ontological Import of Heidegger's Analysis of Anxiety in *Being and Time*. *Southern Journal of Philosophy*, 54(4), 440–62.

McManus, D. (2015). Anxiety, Choice and Responsibility in Heidegger's Account of Authenticity. In *Heidegger, Authenticity and the Self: Themes from Division Two of Being and Time*, edited by D. McManus. London: Routledge, pp. 163–85.

McManus, D. (2019). Affect and Authenticity: Three Heideggerian Models of Owned Emotion. In *Heidegger on Affect*, edited by C. Hadjioannou. Cham: Palgrave Macmillan, pp. 127–52.

McMullin, I. (2006). Articulating Discourse: Heidegger's Communicative Impulse. *Southwest Philosophy Review*, 22(1), 173–83.

McMullin, I. (2013). *Time and the Shared World: Heidegger on Social Relations*. Evanston, IL: Northwestern University Press.

Plato. (1997). *Theaetetus*. Translated by M. J. Levett, revised by Myles Burnyeat. In *Plato: Complete Works*, edited by J. M. Cooper. Indianapolis, IN: Hackett, pp. 157–234.

Polt, R. (2001). The Question of Nothing. In *A Companion to Heidegger's Introduction to Metaphysics*, edited by G. Fried & R. Polt. New Haven, CT: Yale University Press, pp. 57–82.

Polt, R. (2006). *The Emergency of Being: On Heidegger's Contributions to Philosophy*. Ithaca, NY: Cornell University Press.

Polt, R. (2011). Meaning, Excess, and Event. *Gatherings: The Heidegger Circle Annual*, (1), 26–53.

Ratcliffe, M. (2002). Heidegger's Attunement and the Neuropsychology of Emotion. *Phenomenology and the Cognitive Sciences*, 1, 287–312.

Ratcliffe, M. (2008). *Feelings of Being: Phenomenology, Psychiatry and the Sense of Reality*. Oxford: Oxford University Press.

Ratcliffe, M. (2009). The Phenomenology of Mood and the Meaning of Life. In *The Oxford Handbook of Philosophy of Emotion*, edited by E. Goldie. Oxford: Oxford University Press, pp. 349–71.

Ratcliffe, M. (2010). Depression, Guilt and Emotional Depth. *Inquiry*, 53(6), 602–26.

Ratcliffe, M. (2013). Why Mood Matters. In *The Cambridge Companion to Heidegger's Being and Time*, edited by M. A. Wrathall. Cambridge: Cambridge University Press, pp. 157–76.

Ratcliffe, M. (2015). *Experiences of Depression: A Study in Phenomenology.* Oxford: Oxford University Press.

Ruin, H. (2000). The Passivity of Reason – On Heidegger's Concept of *Stimmung. SATS: Nordic Journal of Philosophy*, 1(2), 143–59.

Sartre, J.-P. (2007 (1938)). *Nausea.* Translated by L. Alexander. New York: New Directions.

Scheler, M. (2010). Reality and Resistance: On *Being and Time*, Section 43. In *Heidegger: The Man and the Thinker*, edited by T. Sheehan. New Brunswick: Transaction Publishers, pp. 133–44.

Schloßberger, M. (2020). Max Scheler. In *The Routledge Handbook of Phenomenology of Emotion*, edited by T. Szanto & H. Landweer. Abingdon, UK: Routledge, pp. 72–86.

Shockey, R. M. (2016). Heidegger's Anxiety: On the Role of Mood in Phenomenological Method. *Bulletin d'Analyse Phénoménologique*, 12(1), 1–27.

Slaby, J. (2010). The Other Side of Existence: Heidegger on Boredom. In *Habitus in Habitat II: Other Sides of Cognition*, edited by S. Flach & J. Söffner. Bern: Peter Lang, pp. 101–20.

Slaby, J. (2014). Affectivity and Temporality in Heidegger. In *Feeling and Value, Willing and Action: Essays in the Context of a Phenomenological Psychology*, edited by M. Ubiali & M. Wehrle. Cham: Springer, pp. 183–206.

Slaby, J. (2017). More than a Feeling: Affect as Radical Situatedness. *Midwest Studies in Philosophy*, 41(1), 7–26.

Slaby, J. (2021). Disposedness (*Befindlichkeit*). In *The Cambridge Heidegger Lexicon*, edited by M. A. Wrathall. Cambridge: Cambridge University Press, pp. 242–9.

Stambaugh, J. (1996). *Being and Time: A Translation of* Sein und Zeit. Albany, NY: State University of New York Press.

Stephan, A. & Walter, S. (2020). Situated Affectivity. In *The Routledge Handbook of Phenomenology of Emotion*, edited by T. Szanto & H. Landweer. Abingdon, UK: Routledge, pp. 299–311.

Stolorow, R. D. (2014). Heidegger, Mood and the Lived Body. *Janus Head*, 13(12), 5–11.

Svenaeus, F. (2000). Das Unheimliche – Towards a Phenomenology of Illness. *Medicine, Health Care and Philosophy*, 3, 3–16.

Vallega-Neu, D. (2019). Truth, Errancy, and Bodily Dispositions in Heidegger's Thought. In *Heidegger on Affect*, edited by C. Hadjioannou. Cham: Palgrave Macmillan, pp. 205–26.

Ward, K. (2021). Breaking Down Experience – Heidegger's Methodological Use of Breakdown in *Being and Time*. *European Journal of Philosophy*, 29(4), 712–30.

Withy, K. (2012). The Methodological Role of Angst in *Being and Time*. *Journal of the British Society for Phenomenology*, 43(2), 195–211.

Withy, K. (2013). The Strategic Unity of Heidegger's *The Fundamental Concepts of Metaphysics*. *Southern Journal of Philosophy*, 51(2), 161–78.

Withy, K. (2014). Situation and Limitation: Making Sense of Heidegger on Thrownness. *European Journal of Philosophy*, 22(1), 61–81.

Withy, K. (2015a). *Heidegger on Being Uncanny*. Cambridge, MA: Harvard University Press.

Withy, K. (2015b). Owned Emotions: Affective Excellence in Heidegger on Aristotle. In *Heidegger, Authenticity and the Self: Themes from Division Two of Being and Time*, edited by D. McManus. London: Routledge, pp. 21–36.

Withy, K. (2019). Finding Oneself, Called. In *Heidegger on Affect*, edited by C. Hadjioannou. Cham: Palgrave Macmillan, pp. 153–76.

Withy, K. (2021a). Anxiety (*Angst*) and Fear (*Furcht*). In *The Cambridge Heidegger Lexicon*, edited by M. A. Wrathall. Cambridge: Cambridge University Press, pp. 37–9.

Withy, K. (2021b). Mood (*Stimmung*). In *The Cambridge Heidegger Lexicon*, edited by M. A. Wrathall. Cambridge: Cambridge University Press, pp. 500–3.

Withy, K. (2021c). Thrownness (*Geworfenheit*). In *The Cambridge Heidegger Lexicon*, edited by M. A. Wrathall. Cambridge: Cambridge University Press, pp. 753–6.

Withy, K. (2021d). We Are a Conversation: Heidegger on How Language Uncovers. In *Language and Phenomenology*, edited by C. Engelland. New York: Routledge, pp. 132–48.

Withy, K. (2022a). Having Some Regard for Human Frailty: On Finitude and Humanity. In *Heidegger and the Human*, edited by I. Farin & J. Malpas. Albany, NY: State University of New York Press, pp. 307–24.

Withy, K. (2022b). *Heidegger on Being Self-Concealing*. Oxford: Oxford University Press.

Wrathall, M. A., ed. (2021a). *The Cambridge Heidegger Lexicon*. Cambridge: Cambridge University Press.

Wrathall, M. A. (2021b). Affordance (*Bewandtnis*). In *The Cambridge Heidegger Lexicon*, edited by M. A. Wrathall. Cambridge: Cambridge University Press, pp. 31–3.

The Philosophy of Martin Heidegger

About the Editors

Filippo Casati

Lehigh University

Filippo Casati is an Assistant Professor at Lehigh University. He has published an array of articles in such venues as *The British Journal for the History of Philosophy*, *Synthese*, *Logic et Analyse*, *Philosophia*, *Philosophy Compass* and *The European Journal of Philosophy*. He is the author of *Heidegger and the Contradiction of Being* (Routledge) and, with Daniel O. Dahlstrom, he edited *Heidegger on Logic* (Cambridge University Press).

Daniel O. Dahlstrom

Boston University

Daniel O. Dahlstrom, John R. Silber Professor of Philosophy at Boston University, has edited twenty volumes, translated Mendelssohn, Schiller, Hegel, Husserl, Heidegger, and Landmann-Kalischer, and authored *Heidegger's Concept of Truth* (2001), *The Heidegger Dictionary* (2013; second extensively expanded edition, 2023), *Identity, Authenticity, and Humility* (2017) and over 185 essays, principally on eighteenth to twentieth-century German philosophy. With Filippo Casati, he edited *Heidegger on Logic* (Cambridge University Press).

About the Series

A continual source of inspiration and controversy, the work of Martin Heidegger challenges thinkers across traditions and has opened up previously unexplored dimensions of Western thinking. The Elements in this series critically examine the continuing impact and promise of a thinker who transformed early twentieth-century phenomenology, spawned existentialism, gave new life to hermeneutics, celebrated the truthfulness of art and poetry, uncovered the hidden meaning of language and being, warned of "forgetting" being, and exposed the ominously deep roots of the essence of modern technology in Western metaphysics. Concise and structured overviews of Heidegger's philosophy offer original and clarifying approaches to the major themes of Heidegger's work, with fresh and provocative perspectives on its significance for contemporary thinking and existence.

For EU product safety concerns, contact us at Calle de José Abascal, 56–1°,
28003 Madrid, Spain or eugpsr@cambridge.org.

www.ingramcontent.com/pod-product-compliance
Ingram Content Group UK Ltd.
Pitfield, Milton Keynes, MK11 3LW, UK
UKHW021110100725
460633UK00016B/238